Presented To:

Lialita Johnson

From:

Date:

Feb 21, 2012

DREAMS &
SUPERNATURAL
ENCOUNTERS

DREAMS & SUPERNATURAL ENCOUNTERS

AN INVITATION FOR EVERYONE TO EXPERIENCE GOD

JULIE MEYER

This book and all other Destiny Image, Revival Press, Mercy Place, Fresh Bread, Destiny Image Fiction, and Treasure House books are available at Christian bookstores and distributors worldwide.

For a U.S. bookstore nearest you, call 1-800-722-6774.
For more information on foreign distributors, call 717-532-3040.
Reach us on the Internet: www.destinyimage.com.

ISBN 13 TP: 978-0-7684-3812-3
ISBN 13 Ebook: 978-0-7684-8985-9

For Worldwide Distribution, Printed in the U.S.A.

1 2 3 4 5 6 7 / 15 14 13 12 11

Dedication

I dedicate this book to everyone struggling to just stay on the Ferris wheel of favor—all of you who are in the midst of changing seasons and the many times in this life when you are overlooked, forgotten, demoted, or the favor of God and man seems to have passed you by.

During these times, may your chief joy be the Lamb. May these be some of your favorite times with the Lord. And may you remember to not just endure these seasons but find great joy here—because you get to the front by way of the back, and you get to the top by way of the bottom.

Acknowledgments

First of all, I would like to thank Walt, my husband of 25 years, for all of his encouragement, for all of the times he reminded me of my own dreams and of the faithfulness of our glad God. I love you, Walt.

I want to thank my entire, wonderful family—Isaac and Brittany, and our awesome twins, Jesse and Joseph—I am blessed beyond measure to be your mom. My favorite night of the week is family night. So here is to many nights of roast beef, homemade mashed potatoes, noodles, and dump cake.

Mike and Diane Bickle. Here we are after 27 years together—we still like each other, we still crave the presence of God, we are still hungry for more of God, and we are ever-growing as lovers of God. Thank you both for your lives, for your teachings, and for inviting the world to pray. My life was changed the day I heard you say, "I am a lover of God; therefore, I am successful."

Justin and Naomi Rizzo. Thank you for being such a wonderful couple. Justin, it is pure joy to my heart to be part of your International House of Prayer (IHOP) worship team. I love singing about Eden and pondering Revelation 22 together with every team member on their instruments. I love opening the Word of God, flipping through Scripture passages, singing them out, and contemplating eternity.

John and Lori Elwick. Many thanks for opening your wonderful home in Colorado Springs so I could hide away and finish this book. What an inspiration you both are to my life.

James Goll. This book would not have come about if not for you. Thank you for your encouragement. Thank you for all the times I sent you dreams and you helped me with their interpretation. Thank you for being a mentor in my life. I am blessed to know you.

Stacey Campbell. I have loved our growing friendship. You make me laugh. You inspire me in the Word. I love your passion for people and for God—whether you are in a big meeting or a small meeting, you are the same. And I sincerely hope that by the time you read these acknowledgments that both of us have wonderful memories of Tuscany.

Graeme and Sabrina Walsh. You will never know the depths to which you have touched my heart and brought joy to my life. How blessed I am to call you my friends. So here is to piles and piles of joy and piles and piles of mercy.

Destiny Image Publishers. I would like to thank everyone at Destiny Image who has helped bring this book to life. I hope to be on this journey with you for many years.

Endorsements

Julie Meyer has the most amazing dreams from the Lord, and she articulates them so well. Whenever I hear Julie share a dream, I am always profoundly impacted. You will love this book and perhaps you will even receive an impartation to dream glorious God-dreams that will transform your life!

Patricia King
XPmedia.com

Acts 2 tells us that in the latter days one of the primary means by which God will speak to His children is through dreams and visions. Julie Meyer is evidence of the Lord's desire to strengthen and encourage His people through prophetic dreams. Julie's encounters with the Lord reveal the tender jealousy of our heavenly Father toward His children. They will encourage you, as they have me personally, in our wholehearted pursuit of the Lord Jesus.

Wesley Hall
Provost, International House of Prayer University
IHOP.org

Julie Meyer's credibility and history in receiving divine dreams and understanding their messages are striking and proven. Every dream she tells in this book, chapter after chapter, has its own unique application that is certain to be relevant to your life. As you read this book, you will gain a clearer perspective on what the Spirit is saying to the church in this hour. Get ready for your heart to burn within you.

Bob Sorge
Author, *Secrets of the Secret Place*

With clarity and accuracy, Julie Meyer brings us truths from the Father's heart that give light for the days in which we live. Her dream life is amazing. Her humility is a reality. Her devotion to Jesus is a model for many! Let the Spirit of Revelation come upon you as you devour the nuggets found in this treasure trove!

James W. Goll
Encounters Network
Prayer Storm and Compassion Acts
Author of *The Seer, The Lost Art of Intercession*
Dream Language, and many more

This chronicle is exhilarating, revelatory, and packed with the essence of the Lord's holiness. The revelatory dream gift that operates through Julie Meyer has impacted many. I have seen it in person, and to now read it is such a blessing—a blessing to the entire Body of Christ! Thank you for releasing this revelation, Julie. The truths contained in these dreams call us all deeper into the revelation of God's power and beauty.

Faytene Kryskow
Revivalist, TheCRY, and MY Canada

I love to read Julie Meyer's dreams. They encourage, inform, and excite me. Not only do they make me want to live, but suddenly I feel like I will thrive. Why? Because I am reading God's heart through Julie. Her book is the book of God's dreams.

Through her dreams, I dream—and those dreams are destined to become reality.

Barbara J. Yoder
Senior Pastor and Lead Apostle, Shekinah Church
Founder and Apostolic Leader,
Breakthrough Apostolic Ministries Network
www.shekinahchurch.org; www.barbarayoderblog.com

I am continually amazed at the level of dreams Julie is having on a consistent basis! As they are read, the life of Heaven can be felt as if we are there ourselves. There really is an impartation released within each message as we take them into our own spirits through reading this book. It brings us to the heart of God in this hour—simply amazing!

JoAnn McFatter
www.JoAnnMcFatter.com

Julie Meyer is a modern-day John the Revelator who sees directly into the purposes of Heaven. Throughout this book, her amazing encounters with God in the realm of her dreams are relayed in such a vivid and detailed way. This book is full of holy revelations and urgent messages from the heart of God. As you read, you will feel the presence of God's glory, the passion of His heart, and you will sense the urgency to tap into the often unexplored territory of dreams. Be uplifted, be encouraged, and be inspired to dream!

Joshua and Janet Angela Mills
Prophetic Revivalists
New Wine International, Inc.
Palm Springs, California

Julie Meyer is well-known and much loved for her prophetic worship and her unique ability to draw us into the very presence and glory of God. Her revelatory encounters with the spirit realm are evident through her anointed music. In this, her second book, she recounts and retells her prophetic dreams and experiences in the heavenly Kingdom, and we get to glimpse the heavens through her eyes. Be ready to see your desire for intimacy with the Lord ignited and fueled with fresh fervency by Julie's book!

Jane Hansen Hoyt
President/CEO
Aglow International

Julie Meyer is one of the most trustworthy prophets I know. Her revelation is saturated with scriptural truth, and the Word comes alive in her dreams. I find myself continually challenged to go deeper with God when I read what the Lord has given her. Best of all, her day life is consistent with her night life. Julie is a true lover of God; therefore, He trusts her with His secrets. Her dreams will build up your faith, stir your heart to love God, and fill you with hope. We highly recommend this book.

Wesley and Stacey Campbell
www.beahero.org
www.revivalnow.com

It has been my observation through the years that Julie Meyer has consistently captured God's heart for our day by her revelatory insights, which she has conveyed with a credible and relevant voice in her writings and prophetic worship. In his epistle to the Colossians, the apostle Paul clearly outlined the New Testament strategy of excavating the treasures of wisdom and knowledge hidden in Christ and conveying them to the Lord's people through the written Word and also through psalms, hymns, and spiritual songs. That admonition is clearly captured in Julie's ministry and her new book *Dreams and Supernatural Encounters*. A modern-day spiritual army is being prepared and positioned for the greatest outpouring of God's Spirit ever witnessed. The insightful revelations contained in this book will serve as a spiritual blueprint to help position each reader for his or her place in that incredible destiny.

Paul Keith Davis
Founder, White Dove Ministries

Through the pages of this book, you're invited into the inner chambers of Julie Meyer's relationship with God. Each dream is a treasure carrying the presence of God and a spirit of revelation. Allow the Holy Spirit to awaken your dream life as you hear the hidden mysteries of Christ revealed to Julie.

Ché and Sue Ahn
Senior Pastors, HRock Church

A must-read! I stepped into the living prophetic end-time message where the Bridegroom is calling His Bride into a greater place of holiness and intimacy.

Nonnie McVeigh
National President, Aglow International
Britain

Julie Meyer has done it again—the dreams recorded here have provoked my heart into deeper places of longing for and seeking after the presence of the Lord. The dreams are rooted in biblical reality and challenge me to make room in my worldview for the spiritual realm to become more and more real to me. My heart is encouraged, my mind is challenged, and my longing for Jesus has increased. That's a book worth the price!

Gary Wiens
Director, International House of Prayer Northwest
Author, *Bridal Intercession* and *Come to Papa*

Julie Meyer's pure and childlike relationship with Jesus imparts to the reader a rich appreciation for the heart of God and His presence. She is thrilled with the prospect of His love and power saturating the world of media and anointing His saints with supernatural creativity. Her fervor goes on to rivet our attention on the richest pillars of our faith, accented by the revelations of her true prophetic gift. She is the real deal, and will bring encouragement and joy to many.

Heidi Baker, PhD
Founding Director
Iris Ministries
October 2010

Julie is truly a gifted dreamer. I would call her a master dreamer. She has written this book out of her own dreams and visions. If you are wanting to learn how to prophesy and pray with your dreams this is the book for you. It is her dreams and visions put to pen, and as you read you will see how God can put you on like a glove and use you even as you are dreaming.

Beni Johnson
Bethel Church

But Jesus called them to Himself and said, "You know that the rulers of the Gentiles lord it over them, and those who are great exercise authority over them. Yet it shall not be so among you; but whoever desires to become great among you, let him be your servant. And whoever desires to be first among you, let him be your slave—just as the Son of Man did not come to be served, but to serve, and to give His life a ransom for many" (Matthew 20:25-28).

Contents

Foreword

Julie Meyer and I have been friends since she was a college student. I first met her when she sang for the youth group of the church I was pastoring in St. Louis, Missouri. She was young and still growing in the prophetic, but her voice was anointed. I knew the Lord was going to do something special with her and use her to touch the nations.

Over the years, I have seen her mature spiritually and become more confident in her prophetic singing. She sings to God and from God, and has blessed many through her singing ministry. In the last few years, she has begun to cultivate her prophetic gifting in relation to the dreams she has received from the Lord. Many others would become puffed up with pride if they were given such dreams. Julie stewards her dreams and prays them faithfully, aware of the responsibilities the Lord has given her.

Julie's prophetic dreams are given in the context of her commitment to walk in humility in her relationship with Jesus. I have watched her go through seasons of promotion and demotion and come out unoffended. In each encounter she has had with the Lord, she seeks to die to herself and to grow in the knowledge of God. She has gone on a journey of prayer and humility. I value these prophetic dreams because they extend to us an invitation to go on that same journey of humility. The joy that Julie has found is available to you, because everyone can encounter the Lord. Everyone can pray, pursue intimacy, and seek Him. His desire is for us to know Him and to be with Him where He is (see John 17:24).

I pray that you will meet Jesus in a profound way as you read this book. God is looking for those who will hear what He is saying to the Church in this hour of history and will respond in prayer, asking for His will to be fulfilled and seeking His face. He is looking for friends who will humble themselves before Him in worship, who will find joy in the lowest places, and who are willing to go on this journey with Him. No matter what your circumstances, the invitation to encounter is open to all.

The Lord has given Julie Meyer many prophetic dreams over the years that have brought insight and encouragement to me and many others. The Scripture testifies that God has spoken to His people through prophetic dreams throughout history and that in the last days the Spirit will release prophetic dreams to many (see Joel 2:28-29; Acts 2:17-18). I believe that you will receive understanding and strength from the Lord as you read through the amazing dreams that the Lord has given Julie.

Mike Bickle
Director of the International House of Prayer
Kansas City, Missouri

Preface

Throughout this book I share some of my very favorite of the many dreams I have had. God has shown me in these dreams how He perceives our struggles and that every single choice counts. We are in His gaze. He is watching everything from the biggest choice to the smallest. Everything is seen and captured in His gaze. It is written in His Book. All of those seasons in our lives when we feel we are overlooked and left out—those are God's favorite times with us.

I believe these dreams will be keys to help you see yourself differently in the midst of the process as God works on heart issues. May you be encouraged to *love* the "me and God alone" times. It all counts with God. With these dreams, I give you points on how to pray for the season of life you are in and also for the people living in the city and region where you live.

My hope is that this book will stir your desire to ask the Lord for dreams and for visions and encounters. James 4:2 says, *"...You do not have because you do not ask."* Sometimes it is as easy as asking, "God, what are You thinking? What are You feeling, God?" But be encouraged that He has also made us a promise to pour out His Spirit as seen in Acts 2.

I pray that reading through these dreams will stir your heart more and more, and that you will know that God is listening, and God is available. He is not too busy to hear your requests and your prayers. He is reigning, and He alone is sitting on the throne. This is the God who answers our prayers (see Gen. 28:20). So ask and keep on asking for what you believe is His will for you. It is His personal promise to His children, as He said in James 4. Then write down all of the blessings He gives you. Be faithful with what He gives to you, and He will always give more.

I also want to encourage you to begin to bring your dreams to the Lord in intercession. When the Lord reveals something to you in the night, that is the time to labor with the Great Intercessor Himself and pray for God's purposes on the earth. What did He show you? What did He reveal to you? Bring these things before the Lord in prayer and watch God act and move.

> *For since the beginning of the world men have not heard nor perceived by the ear, nor has the eye seen any God besides You, who acts for the one who waits for Him* (Isaiah 64:4).

First, before I begin describing my dreams, I take a step back into the Bible and lay the foundation for dreams—past, present, and future. As you read, keep in mind that you are part of what God has in store for all who believe in Him.

Introduction

But as it is written: "Eye has not seen, nor ear heard, nor have entered into the heart of man the things which God has prepared for those who love Him." But God has revealed them to us through His Spirit. For the Spirit searches all things, yes, the deep things of God (I Corinthians 2:9-10).

For years, my desire has been to pursue the knowledge of the Lord. I want to understand the things of God in a deeper way. Many times I have personalized First Corinthians 2:9-10 and prayed it over and over: "God, let my eyes see, let my ears hear that which You have prepared for me. Send Your Spirit to reveal the deep things of Your heart to me. What are you thinking? What are Your thoughts toward me, toward my family, and for this nation? Spirit of God, reveal what my mind cannot understand on its own."

God is beyond demonstration or definition. Our human minds cannot fully understand Him. Yet He longs for us to know Him, and so He has made a way for us to know Him by giving us the Holy Spirit. The knowledge of God is within the reach of even the weakest among us with the Spirit's guidance. The Spirit searches out the deepest parts of the Godhead and then reveals to us what He finds.

I imagine the knowledge of God as a vast ocean. The Holy Spirit is like a giant searchlight shining into that ocean to reveal God to us: His character, His attributes, His emotions, and mysteries hidden away since the foundation of the earth. The Spirit reveals to us what our natural minds could never comprehend on their own. As we explore the knowledge of God, He guides us deeper until, suddenly, we see a glimmer of revelation. Each glimpse given to us enlightens our understanding to the glad heart of God and the passionate joy of Jesus Christ.

This revelation comes as we join with the Spirit in various ways. Sometimes He meets us as we study and meditate on the Word, serve others, pray, and work with an excellent spirit. Other times He meets us in dreams, as He met Jacob, Solomon, Daniel, Joseph, and many others in the Bible. All are opportunities to give ourselves fully to the Lord. For just as the Holy Spirit searches out the Godhead and reveals hidden things to us, He is simultaneously searching out the deepest parts of us and revealing our hidden thoughts and motives to God. As we say, "God, I want more of You in my life," God's answer to us is, "Yes, you can have more of Me, but I want more of you."

Revelation 4 is a powerful picture of surrender and heavenly humility. The 24 elders encircling the Lord's throne continually cast their crowns—their worth and all that they are—before the eternal God. They go low before Him, bowing down over and over.

This reality is not for them alone. God wants to make us great on the inside, bringing us into our eternal spiritual identity as humble worshipers of Him. The Lord is giving us an open invitation to join the elders in humbling ourselves before Him.

> *After these things I looked, and behold, a door standing open in heaven. And the first voice which I heard was like a trumpet speaking with me, saying, "Come up here, and I will show you things which must take place after this"* (Revelation 4:1).

So how do we respond to this open door? We must realize that it is an opportunity for us to seek to understand God's heart and to walk humbly in all seasons of our lives. God is asking for humility to reign in the hearts of His people; by this we will show Jesus Christ as glorious as He truly is. He is asking us to go low like the elders.

SHARING MY DREAMS

I have given myself to seeking God, and in the process I have had many dreams. I want to share these dreams because they are not just personal dreams; they are open to whoever has ears to hear. I believe they contain truths from the Lord for the entire Church and an invitation for all believers. As you read, put yourself into these dreams and let the Holy Spirit draw you into an encounter with Him.

The truths spoken in these dreams give us vivid pictures of how the Lord sees all believers and what He desires from each of us. He is looking for friends who will hear His invitation and go on the journey of humility before Him—those who will intercede with Him and who will love Him regardless of their life circumstances or positions.

If you set your heart to take this journey with the Lord, no matter what positions you may hold in life, He will meet you.

As you read through these dreams, keep a few things in mind. First, God promotes and demotes, and everything is backward in His Kingdom. He moves one to the front and another to the back, although He loves them both the same. Regardless of the position you hold, He is fashioning your heart to love Him fully. In every season of your life, God is looking for your heart to be abandoned to loving Him, whether you are shining in the front or hidden in the back.

We can find great joy in being at the back of the line and even in being demoted, for we are strengthened and we encounter the Lord in those times. At other times, God invites us into a night season, asking us to love Him and trust that He will be with us throughout difficult seasons. Everything that happens to us must truly come through God first, and if it comes through God, He has a purpose in it. Through each circumstance, He is again inviting us to love Him wholeheartedly. God is looking for those who love in every season and are faithfully devoted to Him, through pain and through success.

Second, we move God's heart when we are faithful in what little we are given. God helps us climb the mountain of holiness one step at a time; He is with us, for us, cheering us on, and enjoying us every step of our journey. No one is held at bay or left out of this invitation. Even if we will never hold positions of authority or be famous, we can all be faithful with the responsibilities He has given us.

Last, every dream and every sentence is written in hopes that you will pray. Prayer is the simplest thing in the world to do, but it is the thing that is done the least. As a general definition, prayer is agreeing with God. Prayer is one of the primary ways we encounter Him, which leads to becoming like Him. The humble King greatly desires our partnership in agreeing with His heart.

I trust you desire this partnership with God, so join me in a journey into understanding God's heart toward us. We will sit with the Lord, hear His voice, and let Him hear ours. As we seek Him, bow low in humility, and cultivate an unoffended heart at every step, we will wait for Him to pour out His Spirit in astonishing ways.

> *And it shall come to pass in the last days, says God, That I will pour out of My Spirit on all flesh; your sons and your daughters shall prophesy, your young men shall see visions, your old men shall dream dreams. And on My menservants and on My maidservants I will pour out My Spirit in those days; and they shall prophesy* (Acts 2:17-18).

Chapter 1

The Promise of Dreams

But this is what was spoken by the prophet Joel: "And it shall come to pass in the last days, says God, That I will pour out of My Spirit on all flesh; your sons and your daughters shall prophesy, your young men shall see visions, your old men shall dream dreams. And on My menservants and on My maidservants I will pour out My Spirit in those days; and they shall prophesy. I will show wonders in heaven above and signs in the earth beneath: Blood and fire and vapor of smoke. The sun shall be turned into darkness, and the moon into blood, before the coming of the great and awesome day of the

LORD. And it shall come to pass that whoever calls on the name of ·
the LORD shall be saved" (Acts 2:16-21).

I was never one who would really dream. I prayed for dreams.
When I read the Scriptures, I was so encouraged by how God personally talked to the patriarchs of old through dreams, and that
began to stir a deep longing within me to dream His dreams.

I talked to different people who told me of their journeys in
dreams. Some people had wonderful stories of encountering the
Lord as a small child, and from that time on they began to dream.
Some people I talked with felt called as a child to dream and carry
the message of the Lord to the nations, and some even had angelic
encounters. I, on the other hand, had none of these. I didn't dream.
I didn't have angelic encounters. I only had a cry on the inside that
wanted to experience God the way the believers of old did.

In 2000, I began to feel a yearning in the depths of my soul for
more. I wanted a Psalm 27:4 experience. I wanted to gaze on the
beauty of the Lord. I wanted to see His face. I wanted to hear His
voice. I wanted to dream. I wanted to know what was on God's heart
and what He was thinking about. I was consumed with this desire.

I began to ask for dreams. I found myself daily and sometimes
even hourly praying Revelation 4:1:

After these things I looked, and behold, a door standing open in
heaven. And the first voice which I heard was like a trumpet speaking
with me, saying, **"Come up here, and I will show you** *things which*
must take place after this."

I took this Scripture passage seriously, as if the Lord was
speaking straight to me. I asked all the time, "Take me up, Lord.
Show me what must take place. Why not me? Take me up, Lord,
by the divine escort of the Holy Spirit. Take me up and let me see
what You see." Now this is not everyone's journey, but it was mine.
From the year 2000 until June 2004, it was my daily request. I

began to study throughout the Word of God how the patriarchs of old would seek the Lord and dream.

I would pray Revelation 4:1, then go to bed, wake up the next morning, and...nothing. Then the next day, I would do the same thing. Pray Revelation 4:1, go to bed, wake up the next morning, and...nothing. Still, I could not stop asking, night after night, "Lord, this is my request. Take me up, let me see what John saw." Nothing.

THEN ONE MORNING

Then finally, there was *that one morning.* I woke up and realized I had had a dream, a personal encounter with the Lord. I called it "The Beauty of the Myrrh" (shared fully in Chapter 6). I had this dream the day before my friend Mary stepped into eternity to be with the Lord. It was a beautiful encounter and I felt as if I was allowed to watch Mary's journey into the presence of her beloved Lord.

The next dream I had was "The Banquet Table" (told in Chapter 11). The dream I had next was "When Justice Rolls, Get Low" (shared in Chapter 22). The dreams did not stop. They seemed to come in seasons. And to this day they continue because of a simple request. "Jesus, take me up. Show me what is on Your heart."

ACTS 2

I wrote this book to share these dreams that have so greatly encouraged me, my family, my friends, and people around the world. Let's start with a journey into Acts 2.

I love this passage of Scripture. It is a personal promise to us. I have written my name in black ink right beside this Scripture from the apostle Peter given so many years ago. Still today we can set our hearts to receive this promise in a fuller measure until the day of Jesus' return.

This is our promise—that God will pour out His Spirit on *all* flesh. We shall dream and we shall see visions. However, there is still more that we are invited to contend for: That we would prophesy, that we would know and understand what is on the heart and mind of God for these times and these days. That our eyes would see wonders in Heaven and signs on the earth—that these great wonders and signs would precede His coming and the greatest revival in the earth. That whoever calls upon the name of the Lord shall be saved.

We get to be part of this.

Acts 2 is our invitation to join God in His purposes and to cry out for more. The Word of God endures forever. It is timeless; therefore, that which Peter spoke over 2,000 years ago we contend for today as we wait for the full measure of the Spirit to be poured out.

This Scripture passage from Acts 2 is Peter's sermon in Jerusalem when the day of Pentecost had fully come. Peter is quoting from the Book of Joel 2:28-29. However, the words "in the last days" are not found in the Book of Joel. These words Peter prophesied. What a wonderful promise that *in* these last days, the Holy Spirit will rest upon all flesh. It is the promise that the Holy Spirit will fall upon *all*, not just upon the apostolic leaders of movements, not just worship leaders, not just the pastors, not just those in authority—the Holy Spirit will fall upon everyone. This includes you and me.

AN EXCITING PROMISE

God's promise is without regard to gender, age, or social prominence; not only will our sons prophesy, but our daughters shall prophesy also. It is the promise of the manifestation of prophecy, dreams, and visions in a great way. This is an exciting promise. In searching through the Scripture, we can see God touching and using men and women of all ages.

Samuel was in his youth when he began hearing God. David was a young man. But John the apostle received the Book of Revelation when he was in his 90s and banished to the Isle of Patmos. Daniel received his dreams while he was in his 80s. What an awesome thing to be in the latter part of life and have God send an angel to you, like He did to Daniel. The Lord said, *"...you are greatly beloved..."* (Dan. 9:23). Nothing in our lives is unnoticed or out of our Father's gaze. He sees everything even when we do not.

Dreams and visions in the Word of God reach from Genesis through Revelation. The Bible is your guide in every way when searching out God's promise of dreams and visions. As you study the Word, and as we study together in this book, you will find that history was changed because of dreams. Kings of the earth set forth plans and decrees because of dreams. Protection was given in dreams. Strategy was given in dreams. The future was foretold in dreams. Your guidebook for dreams and visions *is* the Word of God.

I LOVE DREAMS

I love dreams. Dreams are when God comes down to us (see Ps. 8:4). Dreams are when God reveals God to us, and all we do is go to sleep. God comes down to our level, to the place where we are and He tells us about Himself or how He feels about something. He will come and reveal His love for us, His heart for us, the future He has for us, and how He really feels about us in every season of our lives.

All we have to do is go to sleep and then be faithful to write our dreams down when we get up in the morning. He comes to us and speaks in our own language. He does not come to us in a

dream and speak Russian or French if we don't know those lan-
guages; rather, He comes to us in dreams and speaks the language
we understand.

However, sometimes the Lord may speak a word or a group of
words to us in another language. For example, the Lord wrote a
Hebrew word in the dreams of a couple of friends of mine. They
did not speak Hebrew, but when they woke up, they remembered
the word and wrote it down. Then they began to talk with the
Spirit of the Lord and search the Scriptures for this word. When
they came upon the meaning of the word it had great significance
in their lives. Scripture says in Proverbs, *"It is the glory of God to conceal
a matter, but the glory of kings is to search out a matter"* (Prov. 25:2).

Sometimes we need to do some homework. The Holy Spirit is
the greatest teacher, and He will get our attention in any way He
can to speak a message in a way that we will remember for the rest
of our days on this earth. John says that the Holy Spirit will teach
you all things (see John 14:26).

It is important to remember dreams because God is telling us
His secrets. We can awake in the morning with a clear revelation
from God on how to set our hearts to love God, to walk closely
with Him in the midst of different seasons. He will even reveal to
us a new understanding of direction in our lives. Sometimes we
can even see things about ourselves more clearly in a dream state
because when we are sleeping we are not fighting the frequent accusations from the enemy like when we are awake.

TIPS TO REMEMBERING YOUR DREAMS

If you have said, "I don't dream," well, I'm here to tell you
that everyone dreams—but remembering your dreams can be a
different story. I encourage people to keep pencil and paper right
beside their beds and upon awaking from a dream—no matter the
time—to write it down as soon as possible.

I have found that the longer I go into the day without writing down a dream, the more I forget certain details. I always write my dreams down as soon as I get up. If you do not enjoy writing things down right away—as you might need a cup of coffee before you can really get serious about writing—you can also get a small tape recorder to speak your dreams into so none of the details are forgotten. The important thing is to get the dreams written down or recorded. Even Daniel wrote down his dreams:

> ...Daniel had a dream and visions of his head while on his bed. Then he **wrote down the dream**, telling the main facts (Daniel 7:1).

John wrote in Revelation 1:19:

> **Write** the things which you have seen, and the things which are, and the things which will take place after this.

This instruction to John has always gripped my heart. Write it down. As we are asking God to speak to us, we shouldn't be surprised when He does, and then our part is to write it down. Take it seriously, record it. Habakkuk 2:2 says, *"Write the vision...."*

JOURNEY WITH THE HOLY SPIRIT

I also encourage you to take your dreams and actually journey with the Holy Spirit and let Him walk with you through the dreams. What I mean by "journey with the Holy Spirit" is to take dreams seriously. When I have a dream, the first thing I do is write it down or type it into a computer file. Then I take the dream and talk to God about it. I ask the Lord questions: "What are You saying? What is on Your heart? What do You want me to understand?"

I also search the Scriptures and find Scripture references. I look for nouns, verbs, adjectives, and numbers within the dream and then search the Scriptures for these same words. Then I spend time talking to God and let Him talk back to me. I love letting the Spirit of the Lord lead me in a Bible study of a dream the Lord just gave me. When I linger in this place, it is as if the Holy Spirit Himself becomes my teacher and I begin to see the dream from the Lord's point of view.

As I begin to pray through the dream, I receive His heart. When I linger in this place of prayer, it gives the Spirit of God time to actually come and reveal to me what is on His heart. This is how to grow a deeper relationship with the Spirit of God on the inside and learn to hear His voice.

Ask the Lord

When I have a dream, I don't call a friend who is good at dream interpretation. Instead, this is when my prayer time begins, and I ask the Lord for the interpretation. Some of my greatest Bible studies are when the Holy Spirit leads me through Scripture and actually opens my eyes to what I dreamt in the night. These are some of my very favorite times with the Lord. I ask the Lord for His wisdom, for revelation, and for discernment in understanding what He is saying.

Scripture says concerning Daniel:

*As for these four young men, God gave them knowledge and skill in all literature and wisdom; and **Daniel had understanding in all visions and dreams** (Daniel 1:17).*

Take this Scripture and ask God to do the same for you. Daniel further says:

*I thank You and praise You, O God of my fathers; **You** have given me wisdom and might, and have now made known to me what we asked of You, for **You** have made known to us the king's demand (Daniel 2:23).*

Daniel and his friends not only asked God for the interpretation of the king's dream, but they also asked God to reveal the very dream that the king had.

Daniel told the king in Daniel 2:28, *"There is a God in heaven who reveals secrets. . . ."* Daniel called God the Revealer of Mysteries.

So when you dream, write it down and spend some time in mediation and prayer. Ask the Lord to speak to you by His Spirit and give you wisdom and revelation. Ask the Lord to take you on a journey through the Scriptures and reveal His mysteries to you. There is nothing more awesome than God revealing Himself to your own soul and opening your eyes to the mysteries that He speaks to you in the night.

The secret of the LORD is with those who fear Him. . . (Psalm 25:14).

Chapter 2

Dreams and Visions
From Genesis to Revelation

I love going through the Word of God and looking for all of the times God revealed Himself and His heart through dreams. He spoke to people without regard to position or rank. He spoke to kings who were not in covenant with Him. He used whatever means He could to make wrong things right, to stir the depths of the human heart, and to get His message out.

These biblical dreams have greatly impacted my life. Some of these I remember learning about in Sunday school as a child, but I did not realize until much later that these conversations and encounters actually happened in dreams. I encourage you to study these

45

dreams—read them, sing them, let the Lord speak to your heart, and then ask for the Lord to give you dreams.

KING ABIMELECH

The God of Israel revealed Himself to kings who were not in covenant with Him, including King Abimelech.

Let's set up the framework for this passage of Scripture in Genesis 20:1-8 so we can understand the significance of this dream: Abraham and Sarah have journeyed to Gerar. Abraham is fearful that he will be killed because of his wife Sarah's beauty. So he asks Sarah to pretend she is his sister. This is the second time in Scripture that Abraham has asked his wife to do this.

The first time was in Genesis 12:11-20 when Abraham asked his wife to pretend to be his sister, and then Pharaoh took her to his house. God sent plagues upon Pharaoh and his house. The Word of the Lord tells us that God plagued Pharaoh and his house. Pharaoh said to Abraham, *"What is this you have done to me? Why did you not tell me that she was your wife?"* (Gen. 12:18)

So here again in Genesis 20, we find Abraham asking his wife to do the same thing, but this time God chooses a dream to rescue Sarah.

And Abraham journeyed from there to the South, and dwelt between Kadesh and Shur, and stayed in Gerar. Now Abraham said of Sarah his wife, "She is my sister." And Abimelech king of Gerar sent and took Sarah. But God came to Abimelech in a dream by night, and said to him, "Indeed you are a dead man because of the woman whom you have taken, for she is a man's wife." But Abimelech had not come near her; and he said, "Lord, will You slay a righteous nation also? Did he not say to me, 'She is my sister'? And she, even she herself said, 'He is my brother.' In the integrity of my heart and innocence of my hands I have done this." And God said to him in a dream, "Yes, I know that you did this in the integrity of your heart. For I also withheld you from sinning against Me; therefore I did not let you touch her. Now therefore, restore the man's wife; for he is a prophet, and he will pray for you and you shall live. But if you do not restore her, know that you shall surely die, you and all who are yours" (Genesis 20:1-7).

In this dream encounter, we see several things. God and Abimelech, king of the Philistines, are *talking* and *communicating* to each other—all within a dream. Though this king is not in covenant with the God of Israel, still God reveals Himself as God to Abimelech in this dream. God gives Abimelech notice of his danger. God says to him *"Indeed you are a dead man."*

In this dream, God tells Abimelech that Sarah is another man's wife. God reveals that He is the One who kept Abimelech from sinning. In this dream, God is protecting Sarah. Then Abimelech communicates and *talks back to God.* He is defending himself, saying, *"Did he not say to me, 'She is my sister'?"* Then God gives Abimelech instruction in this dream about what he must do. God tells Abimelech to give Sarah back to Abraham and that Abraham will pray for him; then God promises healing.

This whole conversation took place in a dream. When Abimelech awoke, he obeyed the God of Abraham and heeded this warning. He arose early in the morning and obeyed the instructions given to him by God. He told all of his servants everything that was spoken in the dream and they were "very much afraid." So Abraham prayed to God and God healed them and they bore children, for the Lord had closed up all the wombs of the house of Abimelech because of Sarah, Abraham's wife (see Gen. 20:8-18).

When I read this Scripture, I am stirred by the Lord with the knowledge that God can reveal Himself to anyone, anywhere, and at anytime. This is a perfect example of the importance of praying for the leaders of our nations to encounter the Lord—for God reveals Himself to the righteous and the unrighteous alike.

JACOB

God also revealed Himself to Jacob in a dream:

Now Jacob went out from Beersheba and went toward Haran. So he came to a certain place and stayed there all night, because the sun had set. And he took one of the stones of that place and put it at his head, and he lay down in that place to sleep. Then he dreamed, and behold, a ladder was set up on the earth, and its top reached to heaven; and there the angels of God were ascending and descending on it. And behold, the LORD stood above it and said: "I am the LORD God of Abraham your father and the God of Isaac; the land on which you lie I will give to you and your descendants. Also your descendants shall be as the dust of the earth; you shall spread abroad to the west and the east, to the north and the south; and in you and in your seed all the families of the earth shall be blessed. Behold, I am with you and will keep you wherever you go, and will bring you back to this land; for I will not leave you until I have done what I have spoken to you" (Genesis 28:10-15).

This is an incredible passage. This is not just a nice story; this is our biblical history of God speaking to weak people in dreams and revealing His greatness with promises of mercy and protection. When we find Jacob, he is running for his life as Esau, his brother, had set it in his heart to kill him. Jacob had deceived his father and been blessed with the blessing of the firstborn.

I believe Jacob is in a place of great weakness. He had lied to his father and is running for his life. On his way from Beersheba to Luz, when evening comes upon him, he lies down on very hard ground. He pulls a stone over and uses that hard stone for his pillow and probably gazes up at the stars until sleep finds him.

What was Jacob thinking that very night as he lay on that cold, hard ground? I wonder if he was thinking about the deeds of the day. I wonder if he was thinking about the family he had left, or if he was thinking about the way he lied to his father and pretended to be the brother he was not.

Yet even this night, Jacob, in all his failure, is in the gaze of God's eyes. This night God is planning to make His appearance to Jacob; the same God who spoke to his father will now reveal Himself to Jacob as his "father's God." This night Jacob will take ownership of the very word *God*.

This night Jacob has a dream. He sees a ladder that reaches from earth to Heaven, the angels ascending and descending upon it, and God Himself at the head of it. Jacob sees the divine intervention of God. He sees there is constant communication between Heaven and earth. The councils of Heaven are executed on earth, and the actions and affairs of this earth are all known in Heaven. Angels are employed as ministering spirits to serve all the purposes and designs of Providence, and the wisdom of God is at the upper end of the ladder, directing all the motions. The angels are active spirits, continually ascending and descending; they rest not, neither day nor night, from service, according to the posts assigned them. They ascend to give account of what they have done and to receive orders, and then they descend to execute the orders they have received.[1]

> Then Jacob awoke from his sleep and said, "Surely the LORD is in this place, and I did not know it." And he was afraid and said, "How awesome is this place! This is none other than the house of God, and this is the gate of heaven!" (Genesis 28:16-17).

Jacob *saw* with his eyes direct communication between Heaven and earth. He saw God at the top of the stairs, watching and listening, and then Jacob began to talk to God. Jacob began to pray. What if Jacob was actually seeing a picture of what prayer looks like? For Jacob saw that God was listening and acting on behalf of those who call out to His Name (see Isa. 64:4). God was sending out His heavenly host from the midst of His throne. What if Jacob was seeing a real picture of what Matthew 6:9-13 looks like—when Jesus taught His disciples to pray? For Jacob saw his Father who is in Heaven, and he saw that God is holy.

This passage of Scripture has helped me in my prayer times. I don't picture myself alone praying in a room; rather, I see myself before the very throne of God. I am right before Him, and God is listening. I put myself right in this passage and know that God is sending out His angelic messengers at the sound of my voice.

JOSEPH

We know that Joseph dreamed his dream as a young boy of around 17 years of age (see Gen. 37:5-11). Joseph dreamed two dreams that foretold the future, but seemingly the total opposite happened.

Describing Joseph, one commentator says:

> He was loved and hated, favored and abused, tempted and trusted, exalted and abased. Yet at no point in the one-hundred-and-ten-year life of Joseph did he ever seem to get his eyes off God or cease to trust him. Adversity did not harden his character. Prosperity did not ruin him. He was the same in private as in public. He was a truly great man.[2]

Joseph's whole life was led by dreams. Joseph had a dream, and he told his brothers. His brothers did not take to kindly to the words of Joseph's dream, and Scripture tells us they hated him even more for this dream. Some dreams probably ought not to be shared, especially if the Lord shows you in a dream that you are going to reign over family members!

Then Joseph had another dream in which he saw the sun, moon, and eleven stars bowing down to him—he shared that with his family as well. His brothers got all the more angry at Joseph. Scripture tells us that his father rebuked him but *"kept the matter in mind,"* meaning he began to ponder the dream in his heart (see Gen. 37:11).

The Lord was showing Joseph his future, but—for a season—the exact opposite happened in his life. When Joseph told his family the dream, they all understood it. That is why the brothers got so angry. In that instant, God opened the eyes of their hearts and they all understood the dream, and they became angry at Joseph. So his brothers plotted to get rid of him. Joseph was sold by his brothers into slavery to the Ishmaelites for 20 shekels of silver. They took Joseph to Egypt and sold him to Potiphar, an officer of Pharaoh and captain of the guard. (See Genesis 37:18-36.) Joseph was 17 years of age.

Scripture tells us that the Lord was with Joseph and he was a successful young man. This is very important, as Joseph did not have an angry countenance. He was not bitter. He was not moping around saying, "Why me?" He was not angry at God for the way his life was unfolding. I do not read anywhere in Scripture that Joseph hated his brothers or that he was offended at his circumstances; instead, Scripture tells us that he was successful and had favor. Joseph must have learned at a young age to trust in all the words of the Lord even when things did not look good. (See Psalm 139; 75:6-7.)

We can learn from Joseph and his dreams: if God has given you a dream and the exact opposite happens, trust in the God of

Psalm 139. Joseph had those dreams to hang on to when again his life took a turn for the worse as Potiphar's wife lied to her husband regarding Joseph, and he was cast into the prison where the king's prisoners were confined. Still the Word of the Lord says, *"But the LORD was with Joseph and showed him mercy, and He gave him favor in the sight of the keeper of the prison"* (Gen. 39:21).

THE BUTLER AND BAKER

In this next portion of Scripture, Genesis 40:1-19, Joseph is not the one dreaming the dreams; he is the one who interprets them. The king's butler and baker had been put into prison where they each had a dream. When they arose in the morning, they were sad. I find it interesting that the Word says that they were sad because there was no one to interpret their dreams. They had each dreamed dreams that no one could understand and no official interpreter of dreams was available.

Joseph shows them the direction they need to look and answers them in confidence saying, *"Do not interpretations belong to God?"* (Gen. 40:8). In this season of Joseph's life, he is ready and willing and knows God is the One who interprets dreams. Joseph is given the interpretation of both dreams, and these dreams come to pass as he predicts. Joseph makes only one request to the butler—*"Remember me when it is well with you. . .make mention of me to Pharaoh, and get me out of this house"* (Gen. 40:14). This is the only time we see Joseph mention being in the dungeon and proclaiming his innocence. He simply says, "Remember me."

As we read on in Scripture, we see in Genesis 41:1-8 that at the end of two full years, Pharaoh had two dreams. In the morning, his mind was troubled, so he sent for all the magicians and wise men of Egypt. Pharaoh told them his dreams, but no one could interpret them for him.

Then Joseph is remembered. Pharaoh sends for Joseph and brings him quickly out of the dungeon. Joseph goes from prison to the palace in one day, from the pit to the pedestal. (See Genesis 41:14-40.) And because his heart was not angry in the midst of his circumstances of having to go lower and lower still, Joseph found God in the place where he was and the secrets of the Lord were spoken to him. Joseph points Pharaoh to God when he says, *"It is not in me; God will give Pharaoh an answer of peace"* (Gen. 41:16).

Joseph interprets the king's dream, and his dream saves a nation! God reveals to Joseph what is getting ready to take place and how to survive the coming years. In *one day* Joseph comes up out of prison, uncomplaining and unoffended, and becomes second in command to Pharaoh. After 13 years in prison, Joseph is free.

Over the next several years, Pharaoh saw all his dreams come to pass, and Joseph was reunited with his brothers. What he said to them is an awesome declaration, *"It was not you who sent me here, but God..."* (Gen. 45:8).

Solomon

In First Kings 3:5-14, the Lord appeared to Solomon during the night in a dream and said, *"Ask for whatever you want Me to give you"* (I Kings 3:5 NIV). Solomon said:

> *"So give Your servant a discerning heart to govern Your people and to distinguish between right and wrong. For who is able to govern this great people of Yours?" The Lord was pleased that Solomon had asked for this. So God said to him, "Since you have asked for this and not for long life or wealth for yourself, nor have asked for the death of your enemies but for discernment in administering justice, I will do what you have asked. I will give you a wise and discerning heart, so that there will never have been anyone like you, nor will there ever be. Moreover, I will give you what you have not asked*

*for——both riches and honor——so that in your lifetime you will have
no equal among kings. And if you walk in My ways and obey My
statutes and commands as David your father did, I will give you a
long life"* (1 Kings 3:9-14 NIV).

When Solomon awoke, he realized it had been a dream.

God reveals Himself to Solomon in a dream. God visits Solomon in this dream. All Solomon did was go to bed, and he has an unbelievable encounter with God. They are both talking to each other in this dream. In the midst of dreaming this dream, Solomon's speech and request please the Lord. He is *sleeping,* yet he makes a request to God that does not concern riches or power but wisdom——and God loves his request.

So in this dream, God answers Solomon's request and gives him all that he asked for and also all that he did not ask for. God rewards Solomon in a dream because he asked for something greater than worldly favor and riches. He asked for a discerning heart to govern the people God had given him and it truly moved the heart of God.

DREAMS IN THE BOOK OF DANIEL

We know that Daniel was taken into captivity as a young teen. The first chapter of Daniel reveals how this young man set his heart before God in the middle of a life much like Joseph's life——and here again we find God speaking to kings and giving leadership through dreams.

*In the second year of his reign, Nebuchadnezzar had dreams; his
mind was troubled and he could not sleep. So the king summoned the
magicians, enchanters, sorcerers and astrologers to tell him what he
had dreamed. When they came in and stood before the king, he said
to them, "I have had a dream that troubles me and I want to know*

what it means. ...this is what I have firmly decided: If you do not tell me what my dream was and interpret it, I will have you cut into pieces and your houses turned into piles of rubble. But if you tell me the dream and explain it, you will receive from me gifts and rewards and great honor. So tell me the dream and interpret it for me" (Daniel 2:1-3;5-6 NIV).

I am greatly encouraged by this event because Nebuchadnezzar was the king of Babylon. He was an unrighteous king to whom God spoke in a dream about upcoming events.

Although Nebuchadnezzar had a dream, he could not remember the dream. The Word says that his mind was troubled and he could not sleep. It was as if the Lord stirred him up, which brought great unrest to his heart so that he could not remember this dream. Still, he was greatly troubled by this dream, and he wanted his interpreters to tell him the dream and then interpret it for him. He was so troubled by this dream that he called for all the wise men of the kingdom, and if they could not tell him the dream and its interpretation, he was going to cut them all into small pieces.

All of the wise men in the kingdom said, "There is no one who can do this," and so one by one, Nebuchadnezzar orders that all of the wise men of Babylon are to be killed. (See Daniel 2:10-13.) That is, until Daniel hears of this decree.

Daniel says, "Wait, not so fast." He asks for time, and then he tells his three friends, Hananiah, Mishael, and Azariah, of this dire situation. He asks them to call upon the name of the Lord and plead for mercy concerning the king's dream mystery. (See Daniel 2:14-18.)

Daniel 2:19 (NIV) tells us, *"During the night the mystery was revealed to Daniel in a vision...."* Daniel gives all glory to God saying:

Praise be to the name of God forever and ever; wisdom and power are His. He changes times and seasons; He sets up kings and deposes them. He gives wisdom to the wise and knowledge to the discerning. He reveals deep and hidden things...You have made known to us the dream of the king (Daniel 2:20-23 NIV).

The Lord reveals to Daniel the dream that the king had and the meaning of the dream, and Daniel is taken before the king. Oh, the beauty of the words that flow from his mouth before the king. I love the words that Daniel declares in verse 28, *"There is a God in heaven who reveals mysteries. He has shown King Nebuchadnezzar what will happen in days to come...."* Then Daniel begins to reveal line by line what is going to happen in their nation.

The end result was that Daniel also was able to set things in place to help the nation survive a great famine. He was also promoted by Nebuchadnezzar, king of Babylon. Daniel had high favor with the king all because he was able to tell the king the dream that the king could not remember and then he interpreted the dream.

This is like our president—or another world leader—having a dream, waking up in the middle of the night, then not totally being able to remember the dream. He becomes so troubled by this that he is not able to sleep, so he calls for someone to reveal what the dream means. Then he takes *action* based on the dream's interpretation. Oh, how we should take these words to heart and begin to pray for the kings, presidents, and world leaders of our nations. Who knows what God will do?

This portion of Scripture in Daniel gives my heart encouragement to pray that God will encounter our leaders in dreams. *Oh God, wake them up. Speak to them; let them become troubled and not be able to sleep. And then, Lord, send Your mouthpieces to them. Send Your Daniels to them for such a time as this, and let Your Word be spoken forth in all boldness and clarity.*

The whole Book of Daniel tells of times and seasons unfolded by God speaking to kings and to Daniel in dreams and night visions. In chapter 4, God spoke to Daniel in a series of what Daniel calls *night visions* when Daniel saw the events of the end times right before his eyes. He saw that which was many years ahead of his time; and as we study this book, we also see how *our* future will unfold and what events will precede the reign of Jesus Christ coming back to earth and setting up His Kingdom forever.

New Testament Dreams and Visions

When we move to the New Testament, we see that the birth of Jesus Christ was preceded by dreams. The Lord spoke to Joseph in a dream and told him not to be afraid to take Mary as his wife (see Matt. 1:20). After the birth of Jesus when King Herod was jealous of the child, the Lord spoke to Joseph again in a dream and told him to flee the place where they were as Jesus was in danger (see Matt. 2:13).

Joseph listened every time and obeyed what he was told in the dreams (see also Matt. 2:19-20).

Paul speaks in Second Corinthians 12:2 (KJV):

*I knew a man in Christ above fourteen years ago, (whether in the body, I cannot tell; or whether out of the body, I cannot tell: God knoweth;) such an one **caught up** to the third heaven.*

Paul was literally *caught up* into a vision, and it was so real that he did not even know if it was *real* or a *vision*. He was caught up, and the Lord showed Him what was on His heart.

Revelation Vision

Then there is my all-time favorite vision: the vision of Revelation, which the apostle John saw as the Revelation of Jesus Christ concerning the end times. John was specifically told 12 times in this book to *write*. When you study the word *write* it means:

- to commit to writing (things not to be forgotten), write down, record.

- used of those things which stand written in the sacred books (of the Old Testament).

- to write to one, i.e., by writing (in a written epistle) to give information, directions.

Write is the Greek word *grapho*. It is a verb, an action word.[3] We find the same word in Habakkuk 2:2 (KJV):

And the LORD answered me, and said, Write the vision, and make it plain upon tables, that he may run that readeth it.

What has greatly impacted me in the dreams and visions of the Old and New Testament is that God is speaking today. God is listening today. God is answering people's questions today. God is giving directions, and men and women are listening to God and communicating with God today.

Our part is to *write it down* and pass on the information that God is giving us in *this* day and this *time* so others may join us in intercession. Then we are co-laboring with Jesus Christ the Great Intercessor and birthing His purposes on the earth.

You number my wanderings; put my tears into Your bottle; are they not in Your book?" (Psalm 56:8).

Sign me up!

ENDNOTES

1. *Mattthew Henry's Commentary on the Whole Bible*: New Modern Edition, electronic database (Peabody, MA: Hendrickson Publishers, 1991).

2. James Montgomery Boice, quoted by David Guzik, Enduring Word Media, 2010. http://www.enduringword.com/commentaries/0137.htm (accessed November 5, 2010).

3. Thayer and Smith, "Greek Lexicon entry for Grapho," *The KJV New Testament Greek Lexicon*, electronic edition. http://www.biblestudytools.com/lexicons/greek/kjv/grapho.html (accessed February 4, 2011).

Chapter 3

The Pathway to Encounters

Humble yourselves in the sight of the Lord, and He will lift you up (James 4:10).

What does it mean to encounter God? Is it only when Jesus appears right in front of our eyes? Can anyone encounter the Lord, or are encounters reserved for those who have positions up front, such as pastors and leaders?

When you encounter someone, you come upon or meet the person. Encounter may be hoped for and desired, but it is unplanned, unexpected, or brief. Encountering God is like that. We cannot force God to meet with us or limit Him. He comes to those He wishes to meet, regardless of their positions, in any way He wants. So many people get frustrated because they're looking for Jesus to appear to them face to face, and they refuse to acknowledge anything less. We miss many simple encounters when the Spirit of the Lord is speaking to us or directing us.

For years I wanted to supernaturally meet God. I wanted to experience Him in a very real and tangible way. I always loved hearing conference speakers relate their encounters with the Lord and how they would be taken up to heavenly places. They would see angels. They would speak to the Lord. I longed for all of that. I would ask God, "Why not me?"

I loved reading the Scriptures about encountering the Lord. I would read them time and again. I would pray them. I wanted to know the mysteries of His heart for us, His thoughts toward us, and the secrets He holds. I figured I could never go wrong if I prayed His Word, so I prayed Revelation 4:1 over and over again.

After these things I looked, and behold, a door standing open in heaven. And the first voice which I heard was like a trumpet speaking with me, saying, "Come up here, and I will show you things which must take place after this."

There is a door open in Heaven, and there is an invitation to come up and encounter God. This is not an order from an unfeeling, uninvolved father or a command from an emotionless superior, but an invitation from Someone who embodies desire. And it is more than an invitation to simply come; it is an invitation to come *up*, to ascend.

The Greek word for *come* is *anabaino*. It is not a one-time action, so it carries a lot of weight. *Anabaino* means to approach, to attain, and to be lifted up, and the word carries the idea of doing it continually. "Repetitive attainment with intensity" might be a good way to say it. The door is open in Heaven for us to come up and keep coming. We do not have to beg God to open the door or to let us come. The door is wide open—almost as if it were not able to close—and the invitation is already in our hands. Our task is to reach.

I knew this Scripture that I had prayed so often had been given to the apostle John. But one day, as we were singing this Scripture at the International House of Prayer in Kansas City (IHOP–KC), I felt a shift happen in my heart. After singing the verse a few times, I began to personalize it for myself. "There is an open door for *me*. *I* will come up."

Something deep inside my soul cried out, "This is for *me*. I want this encounter. I want to go up. I will not stop asking. Whatever I must do to get through this door, take me, God. I'm Yours." From that moment, I began praying this verse from Revelation many times each day. Whenever my eyes opened, whether it was in the middle of the night or mid-morning, this prayer was the first thing out of my mouth, week after week for months on end.

HUMILITY

Little did I realize that the Lord would lead me to this open door through one specific pathway—the pathway of humility. Having humility means so much more than going as low as you can. It means embracing the lowest place and finding great joy there—in the last place, in the place of demotion, and in the place of being overlooked.

Humility—this word embodied the Man Jesus when He walked the earth. Humility is the place of great encounter with Him, and it was my pathway to the door standing open in Heaven.

After I began praying for encounters, I first encountered the Lord through humility. I was sitting in the back row, in the midst of my anger, right after being demoted from my position as a worship leader. I didn't encounter Him in a prayer line, at a conference, or within a tangible swirl of divine activity. No one was praying for me, I didn't see any angels, and I didn't hear any songs from Heaven. It was just the Spirit of the Lord quietly speaking to me as I sat in the back row, enraged at being removed from my position. The doors of Heaven were not thrown wide open for me; instead, He gave me a simple invitation to go on a step-by-step journey in humility.

I was already an experienced worship leader and singer by the time I had come to IHOP–KC. I had led worship and taught at several conferences across the nation, and I was comfortable in my worship style. In the early days of IHOP–KC, we were pioneering a new way to flow together as a team when singing prophetic songs. I struggled with the new style at first. I did my own thing. I didn't like change. A good friend eventually took me aside and said, "You know, Michael Jordan was always a great basketball player. But the Chicago Bulls really started winning when he learned to play with his team." However, I still continued to do my own thing.

One evening, I was leading worship. The next day, one of the leaders asked me to step down from the worship-leading rotation for a season because I didn't involve others in the prophetic singing when I led. I was still allowed to sing on a team but not lead. He wanted me to take some time to learn the worship model. In fact, though he did not know it, the Lord was using him to teach me a valuable lesson in humility.

I must be honest and say I didn't take the news of my demotion well. In fact, I was furious. As I sat in the very back row during a worship set I should have been leading, my heart was seething and my mind was racing a hundred miles a minute. I frantically defended myself with irate whispers, muttering to myself, "I am Julie Meyer! I should not be in the back row. I was made for the front." Each time I would think these thoughts, the words would get louder and louder until I was uncontrollably mad, jealous, envious, and frustrated—all the Christian words for angry. And it was all happening right in the middle of worship. Everything I should not be was at the forefront of my heart. I was not enjoying my new position in the back row one bit.

IN THE BACK

I had read one of Bob Sorge's books, *Dealing with the Rejection and Praise of Man*, and yet there I was...angry about what I saw as rejection. I wanted to be in the front; I *deserved* to be there. As the incense of worship was rising to God, I was yelling at Him on the inside, "I hate the back row! I hate the back row!"

People were walking by me and leaning down to ask, "Julie, why are you in the back? Aren't you supposed to be leading right now?" I would look up at them, shrug my shoulders, and give them a huge, fake smile, while inside I was still yelling, "I hate the back row! Hate it, hate it, hate it!" I had a smile on my face, but I was an exploding volcano on the inside. I was fooling everyone but God Almighty, who sees and knows all (see Ps. 139:1-4).

I still remember the worship song being played by the team that took my spot. "Holy, holy are You, Lord God Almighty. Worthy is the Lamb. Worthy is the Lamb." God, at that exact moment, was getting ready to grace me with the encounter of a lifetime, but I was only focused on me.

All of a sudden—in the midst of my anger, envy, jealousy, pride, and just about every other emotion contrary to the Sermon on the Mount lifestyle I sang about daily and professed to live—an interior whisper broke my concentration.

"I have an idea."

It was piercing, yet gentle. It was tender, yet it arrested my attention. The beautiful inner voice of the Holy Spirit, even in this place, did not condemn me, but repeated His invitation for me to dialogue with Him: "I have an idea."

I remember responding, "Go on..."

"Every time you feel the sting that you are feeling now, embrace it and lean into My goodness. Do not get mad. Trust Me in this place; encounter Me in this place; be lovesick for Me in this place. I will either open the door for you to lead worship again or bring you into something else that you will enjoy just as much."

I sat there and thought about this for a minute. I was so focused on being mad, I didn't even realize I was having an intimate conversation with the Holy Spirit. In my pride and jealousy, the ever-wooing Holy Spirit was leading my prideful heart straight into the heart of God. It still surprises me when I say this, but I was encountering the Lord right in the middle of my temper tantrum.

I remember thinking, *OK, I'm going to do this, but I won't tell anyone. I'll see if it works first. Every time I feel the sting of jealousy and the anger of being overlooked or demoted, I am going to lean into the sting. I am going to love Jesus right in the midst of the sting. I am going to set my heart to find Him when I hurt the most.*

I decided there in the back row (literally) to set my heart to find God and to find the joy of the Lord in the lowest place. I guessed that it was not going to be a short season—that it would take a year or two at the very least—but I decided to accept the invitation anyway. God was inviting me to spend some focused time with Him and I wanted to see what He was going to do in my life.

So I began a step-by-step journey with Him into humility. Now that I had taken the first step, I would be invited to take another, then another. I would never know what the next thing was going to be until after I had taken a step.

A Journey

I knew this journey would not be easy. I never imagined there could be any true joy in the lowest place. I thought joy only happened in the highest places of life, where everything was wonderful, everyone was your friend, and you led worship, preached, or prophesied. Joy comes during good times, or at least that's what I thought. Finding joy in the back row was new to me. But it sure seems that God can do the deepest and greatest work on the inside when He tucks us away underneath the shadow of His wings. I'm sure that on the outside, it didn't look like much was happening, but that was certainly the time in my life when I felt the most change.

God loves to show us what is really in our hearts. So how do we get to see it? Well, when life is normal, when there's nothing amazing or terrible happening, we are pretty settled; that's when we get to coast through our days. But when the mixture within our hearts is shaken up and unsettled, our real thoughts, feelings, and beliefs tend to rise to the surface. Many times this happens by demotion, getting fired, being overlooked, or having no favor while everyone else seems to get all the awards. While your friends were invited to the pastors' luncheon, you were put on the bathroom cleaning crew. While your friends were invited to God's banquet feast, your invitation takes you straight into the dark night of the soul. This is the sting I'm talking about. This is the place of encounter with the living God.

God's purpose is to make us great in Him, not just great for the sake of being great (see John 15:1-17). I have realized that if you are called by God, especially into a leadership position, your training will come in the form of being overlooked, demoted, fired, and having seasons of absolutely no favor at all (see Prov. 3:11-12; 13:24; Heb. 12:1-11). But if you go low, the place of encountering the affections and the secrets of God's heart is right in the middle of the sting—at the end of the line and in the back row.

God knows everything, even down to the moments when we sit and stand back up again. Every single thing we do or think or say—yes, that includes the secret motives and hidden thoughts we can keep from those around us—He knows all of it. The grumbling, complaining, and temper tantrums don't just dissolve somewhere in the atmosphere (see Ps. 139:3-5).

The Spirit of mercy and kindness broke into my life that night in January 2000. In the middle of my total weakness, envy, and anger, He fully wanted an encounter with me. That fact was shocking and alluring all at once. But know this: the kindest voice to ever speak to my heart was the Holy Spirit beckoning me to search out the goodness of God in humility.

In the years since then, this lesson has come back to me a thousand times, and it is never easy. A sting always does *sting*. It always feels personal. It always costs something. But each time I feel that sting, I know what I should do: lean into Jesus and go low.

How will our hearts react when everyone around is given honor, respect, and position while we are ignored? Will we get offended? Will we call a leadership meeting to demand honor? Will we send an email to the person who can change the situation for us? Will we complain to our friends instead of asking them to pray for us? Will we try to clear our names or show others our side of the story? Will we talk badly about other people's character and motives? Will we hope to win everyone who talks with us to our side? Will we let our hurt and anger justify some kind of retaliation? Our hearts should be heavy if these things are true. The weight of what is staring back at us in the mirror should make us want to lean into God and ask for His strength.

Though I had said yes to the Holy Spirit's invitation, I still was having trouble working through all the emotions of being fired by my friend and pastor. Then one day I came across this Scripture:

> *For exaltation comes neither from the east nor from the west nor from the south. But God is the Judge: He puts down one, and exalts another* (Psalm 75:6-7).

I felt like the Holy Spirit was yelling it at me. Man does not set us in our place; the Lord does. God raises up one and removes another (see Dan. 2:20-21). God knows what is in our hearts, and wants us to see what He already knows—that most of us need a lot of help in going low and embracing the lowest place with joy. Of course the Lord uses others to affect our positions, but the result is still the same: He is the One moving us. So it wasn't mainly about what someone else did to me, it was about recognizing God's hand in the midst of my circumstances and responding to His invitation.

GOD'S FAVOR

Experiencing God's favor can be like riding a Ferris wheel. One minute we are up in the light of divine favor and the next we are down in the depths of the shadow. God wants us to find joy in both places. He wants us walking steady when we are up and walking steady when we are down. We should not focus on our position. No matter where we are, even if we are totally out of sight from everyone, God knows how to promote us and how to demote us.

I believe God trains us for greatness the same way He trained King David. Early on, we hear of David tending sheep in the boondocks of Bethlehem. But God whispers a secret about him in First Samuel 13:14: *"...The LORD has sought for Himself a man after His own heart, and the LORD has commanded him to be commander over His people...."*

From tending sheep to becoming the king of Israel, from killing Goliath to being hated and hunted by Saul and his massive army, from reigning in royalty to running for his life time and again, David was constantly on the favor Ferris wheel. Throughout his songs and the stories told about him, we are taken with him every step of the way as he shares his deepest thoughts and groans about life and God. David was promoted to the highest heights and demoted to the lowest lows, but at the end of the day what kept David's heart steady was how intently he focused on the Lord—he made the Lord his "one thing."

One thing I have desired of the LORD, that will I seek: that I may dwell in the house of the LORD all the days of my life, to behold the beauty of the LORD, and to inquire in His temple (Psalm 27:4).

God took David on a journey of great sorrow and joy to learn how to embrace the highest and the lowest places while keeping his heart steady. This is the same journey God has us all on and, at the end of the day, the Lord's desire is that the cry of our hearts would be the same—to be focused on God, our One Thing.

When we are stuck in the low places, joy is not easily faked. In fact, the more we try to fake it, the phonier we become in the long run because our spirits will start to wither. For a while we might be able to pretend around our friends, family, ministry staff, or coworkers, but we cannot pretend with God. *"For the eyes of the LORD run to and fro throughout the whole earth, to show Himself strong on behalf of those whose heart is loyal to Him,"* and God knows the intentions of the heart (2 Chron. 16:9; see Jer. 17:10). God is actively looking for those whose hearts belong solely to Him during times of crushing and demotion (see Ps. 62:5-12).

HIS OPEN INVITATION

Sometimes it is hard to discern His invitation when our life circumstances are very difficult. We may experience loss, rejection, illness, and other hardships. But God promises us that He will never leave us nor forsake us, and His invitation is always open to respond to Him with hearts that are unoffended, even in the midst of great pain. He will take us through the valley of the shadow hand in hand; He will be with us every step of the way (Ps. 23:4). Like Paul, we can desire to know Christ in all seasons, *"That I may know Him and the power of His resurrection, and the fellowship of His sufferings..."* (Phil. 3:10).

No matter what season we are in, the Lord is watching to see what is in the depths of our souls. He wants our souls to cling to Him and allow His right hand to uphold us (see Ps. 63:8). He wants us totally empty of ourselves so He can fill us with the fullness of the knowledge of Him. It is His passion and joy to destroy selfish ambition and pride in us.

Here is the invitation from the Lord: if you want to go up, you have to go low; you have to join Him in understanding the power residing in the lowest place. He left the glory of Heaven and clothed Himself in skin. Jesus described Himself as meek and lowly (see Matt. 11:29). He walked in humility when He was on the earth and, according to Psalm 45, humility is one of the main causes He will take up when He returns. He is not going to look like the reserved child who came the first time, and He will not fulfill the role of the sacrificial Lamb again. The Lion of Judah will have fire in His eyes as He rides forth on behalf of truth, righteousness, and humility when we see Him next.

And in Your majesty ride on triumphantly for the cause of truth, humility, and righteousness...and let Your right hand guide You to tremendous things (Psalm 45:4 AMP).

Although not everyone may meet God in exactly the same way I did, this experience is not only for me; I believe He extends His invitation for everyone to embrace—no matter which season we find ourselves in. Sing for joy in the midst of promotion and sing for joy in demotion—when you are alone in your bed, when no one is looking and it is just you and God alone. No matter where you are in your journey, let it be your invitation to encounter God, your heavenly Father.

Let the saints be joyful in glory; let them sing aloud on their beds (Psalm 149:5).

Chapter 4

Come and Sit Awhile

I love this dream because it is an invitation to all to come and sit awhile with the King of the Ages. Let His kind eyes wash you from the inside out and let His mercy surround you. Jesus wants to share His secrets with His friends, and here is the key—come and sit awhile.

I had a dream. I was sound asleep when I felt someone tap me on the shoulder and wake me up. When I sat up, I saw a man on my left side pointing to the other side of the bed.

I looked to the right and saw Jesus sitting at a round table with an extra chair. He pointed to it and extended an invitation to me, "Come and sit awhile."

While the king is at his table, my spikenard [my life and worship] *sends forth its fragrance* (Song of Solomon 1:12).

I walked over to the table and sat down. I remember noticing how His eyes never left my face. He watched every step I took.

He had an old book in front of Him. This book was large and thick, and it looked like worn, brown leather. It would have been almost square if not for its constant use. The Lord was touching the cover very tenderly and running His fingers around the edges, like the book was dear to Him. It reminded me of the moments during family reunions when the photos of generations past are brought out to show the younger generation. The elders turn the pages carefully, not because the photo albums are old, but because the pictures are precious.

For some time I watched Jesus' face, His countenance full of unspoken emotion as He touched the front of this cherished book. He knew what was in it and was clearly moved. He looked into my eyes and again said, "Come and sit awhile."

He was intent on looking straight into my eyes, and I couldn't look away from His gaze. I was drawn in by Him; everything I had carefully hidden away was opened with one glance.

The Eyes of the Lord

His eyes were shining. The eyes of the Lord looked straight into my soul and caused everything to be laid bare. His gaze is where joy and peace give an open invitation into their home; where all of my hidden sins and hidden places are brought into the light and there is no hiding at all; where I finally understand His love and desire for me—I was drawn in by *those* eyes.

In one glance, I felt deep conviction. In one glance, an overwhelming flood of mercy and delight awakened my heart. In one glance, conviction and mercy met and entwined themselves with each other, causing me to want to run straight to Him as fast as I could and lean into Him. Again He said, "Come and sit awhile."

The King of Creation was at a table with me, like He had nothing else to do but sit and just be...with me.

When Jesus looked down at the book, I noticed its title. He turned it for me to read:

Hidden Secrets of the Ages:
Past, Present, and What Is to Come

I looked into His eyes, and He nodded at me to open it. I could feel the tiny ridges and grooves of the old leather as I touched it. I lifted the heavy cover and glanced at the table of contents. The first one I saw was, *"The End From the Beginning,"* and right underneath the title were the words, *"Come and sit awhile."* I kept reading:

Things Yet to Be Revealed
Come and Sit Awhile
Walking Down the Ancient Paths
Come and Sit Awhile
2 Kings 6:12
Come and Sit Awhile

There were many more chapters, but the Lord reached out His hand, closed the book, and said, "Let's just sit awhile. Let's just sit and know." And we sat there for the rest of the dream. He sat with me all night.

When I woke up in the morning, I knew that I had been with the King at His table all night long.

Chapter 5

I Am Undone

*We move Heaven when God stirs our heart to pray day and night
(see Isa. 62).*

*When we entwine ourselves with His purposes and are faithful to
the invitation to intercede, He acts on behalf of those who wait for
Him. This dream is a picture about how faithfulness, especially in
intercession, moves God's heart (see Ps. 132:3-5).*

I had a dream. An angel took me into the room of a man
who was deep in sleep. We stood together at the foot of his bed
so the angel could show me how this faithful person spent even

his unconscious hours. I could hear the man praying while he was asleep. Every time he would roll over in his bed, he would say, "Abba, here I am. Here I am, Abba. I love You, Abba."

I looked up through the ceiling and saw a vast angelic army. Together the angels seemed like an ocean of brilliant, radiant light. It appeared that they were pulsing and trembling, just waiting to break in. They were waiting to be released by the call of the angel who had led me into the room. He was in great anguish because he earnestly desired to give the call they were all expecting, but he only said one sentence, "It is not quite time yet."

Not Quite Time Yet

I kept looking at the heavenly hosts. I could see ladders. I could see lamps. I could feel the anticipation and how strongly they wanted to break in. The angelic multitude was getting ready to burst in, not with a simple entrance, but with a flood of divine activity. Only this single angel held back the imminent breakthrough.

But it was not quite time for him to release them. There was something yet to be completed before the breakthrough could happen, though I was not shown what it was.

I noticed the Lord standing at the head of the man's bed. I was able to feel His gaze of tender kindness and hear His gentle whisper over the man. He said, "So many people said they would do it, and they never did, but you really did it. You really did it." The Lord's affirming voice, affection, and kindness to the man were due to the man's faithfulness in continual night-and-day prayer, even in the mundane things of life. This man did not seek fame and fortune; he stayed steady, lovesick for God, and unoffended day by day.

A tear came from the corner of the Lord's eye; He was deeply moved by this man's faithfulness. The tear fell in slow motion and broke into a hundred tiny splashes on the man's pillow. It was beautiful to watch. This display of passion was a side of the Lord I had not seen before.

From my vantage point, I noticed that the man's room was as bright as day even in the darkness, because the hosts of Heaven were so close to breaking through. The Lord looked at me and said, "We have heard many pray, 'Take us up.' Instead, tell the faithful ones, 'Heaven is coming down. Heaven is breaking in.'"

The Lord added, "And tell them, I am undone."

Chapter 6

The Beauty of the Myrrh

A wonderful woman in our community named Mary had cancer. While many in our area and around the world were crying out to the Lord for her healing, Jesus took her home—she was healed as she stepped into eternity. I felt like Jesus opened the door in a new way so we could see the power of prayer from an eternal perspective. Sometimes our prayers seem to go unanswered, but they ascend to the heavens where He hears every single one. He bends down to listen.

Psalm 116:1-2 says, "I love the LORD, because He has heard my voice and my supplications. Because He has inclined His ear to me, therefore I will call upon Him as long as I live." Maybe you have had someone like Mary in your life. . .although you were praying for the person's healing, God took him or her home. The Lord assured me, "In a minute you will see the person again, and this dark night is actually filling the bowls that Jesus Christ will pour out on the earth." Oh, the beauty of the myrrh—the prayers of the saints for healing! It is so beautiful and it is so powerful.

I had a dream. I saw Jesus go into Mary's hospital room. It was dark in her room, so I knew it was the night hour (see Song of Sol. 5:2). Mary was surrounded by her family. They were keeping watch over her and praying, but they could not see Jesus. He walked over to Mary and touched her hands. Her whole body was dripping with thick myrrh because her family had covered her in unoffended prayer.

As she sat up in her bed, it was like she sat up in an entirely different world—it was bright, colorful, and radiant—and the myrrh on her body had vanished. She sat up glowing and smiling. All the while, Jesus just looked intently at her. They looked at each other for a moment, and then Jesus turned away. Even without words, I knew I was looking at Song of Solomon 6:5, where Jesus says to His Bride, *"Turn your eyes away from Me, for they have overcome Me. . . ."*

With ease and quickness, Mary sprang up from her bed. She noticed that everything about her body was transformed and immediately knew that she was in a different realm. She looked around the room at her family as Jesus quieted her heart with one whispered phrase, "You will see them all in just a minute." And Mary knew it was true.

IN JUST A MINUTE

For the first time, Mary had a deep understanding of how soon they would all see each other again (see Ps. 90:4). To humans living on this side of time, the days seem long, but in eternity, those earthly days are numbered and seen for how short they truly are. Leaving her family would be like dropping her children off in the nursery when they were young. They cried because they were being separated, because they did not understand she would be back in an hour to pick them up. But she knew exactly when she would return. When Mary stepped into eternity, she had a new concept of time and she knew she would see them again—in just a minute.

Jesus and Mary stood there looking at her family. Mary was so tender and loving as she looked at them from the other side of time. Although they could not hear her, she said to them, "You did good. Well done." I knew she was referring to how they had handled her season of suffering without becoming offended at the Lord. She said to Jesus, "This is my family...just look at them. I am so proud of them." She had a look in her eyes that only a wife and a mom can have; she was overwhelmed with love for her family. She kept saying, "You did good. You did good."

The scene changed, and they both turned to face gently flowing waters and green fields. Mary began running and laughing. She was undeniably free. It was as if she could not run fast enough. Her laughter filled the air as Jesus just stood there and watched her run.

"Come See"

With an excited sparkle in His bright eyes, Jesus said, "Come see." He led Mary by the hand into a giant room in the corridors of eternity. The room contained many bowls that had the appearance of enormous communion chalices. Each one was about 50 feet tall and very wide, with a large, sturdy base that tapered to form a stem. At the top of the stem was a bowl that was as wide as it was deep. The bowls were made of something clear, like glass or diamond, so it was easy to see how full they were from the outside. Some of the bowls had just a little liquid in them and some were about half full, but each liquid had its own color and each bowl had its own purpose. The liquid represented intercession.

The room the bowls were in was very loud. The prayers of the saints on earth echoed in this corridor until they came to rest in the bowls as unified, purified liquid prayers (see Rev. 5:8).

Jesus took Mary to a bowl specifically for healing. When she saw how much liquid was in the bowl, she asked, "What is that?"

"This is liquid myrrh," He answered. The spice was the color of pure gold, like thick, golden lava, and it almost ran over the top of the bowl.

Jesus explained, "It is the prayers of the saints for healing. As the saints were praying for your healing and for many others, their hearts and minds were set to love Me. To the same degree that they leaned into the goodness of the Lord amidst their dark times, their thoughts and prayers were being refined by the fire. They learned how to not be offended. Look, Mary, their prayers are ever before Me—like pure liquid gold—and you had a part in the filling of the bowls.

"Mary, you went your way up the mountain. You said yes to Me even in a dark night, in a time of difficulty. And when an enemy of God invaded your body, you did not open your mouth in offense and anger. Only grace, trust, and faith in the goodness of God proceeded from your mouth. So, for the way you lived when death met you face to face—for willingly laying down your life and leaning into Me without offense—I now give you a crown of honor."

He placed the crown on her head. Then Jesus said, "Mary, watch." He tipped one of the gigantic bowls a little so that some of the golden liquid fell to earth. As it fell, a special joy took hold of Mary; she clapped her hands, laughed, and was so excited because she knew it meant good things.

They bent over and looked at earth together. Great signs and wonders and great healings broke out in the places where the golden liquid fell. "I am giving them a taste," Jesus said, "but the day is coming when the bowls will be fully tipped over and poured out upon the earth."

As she stood looking at the bowl of myrrh, Jesus said, "Mary, you are one of the reasons this bowl is so full. The season of the dark night is working to fill the bowls with prayers from hearts and thoughts that are pure, refined, and lovesick. When prayers come before Me that are full of demands and offense, they do not fill the bowls. But look how full the bowl is with the beauty of the myrrh. This is so beautiful and so powerful! The way you lived and the way you left the earth has caused saints from many nations to lean into Me and pray out of lovesickness without offense…and look, Mary. Look how full the bowl is."

Chapter 7

Pink Slips

God is looking at the hidden motives of our hearts and thoughts. He wants us to go to the lowest place and embrace true humility—and to fully delight in it. The ones who do are the ones on whom He shines His light of favor and gives promotion. He knows exactly how our hearts respond when we are stuck in the back row or in the lowest places.

And He sat down, called the twelve, and said to them, "If anyone desires to be first, he shall be last of all and servant of all" (Mark 9:35).

But when you are invited, go and sit down in the lowest place, so that when he who invited you comes he may say to you, "Friend, go up higher." Then you will have glory in the presence of those who sit at the table with you. For whoever exalts himself will be humbled, and he who humbles himself will be exalted (Luke 14:10-11).

I had a dream. A man was sitting at his desk with a pile of phone messages in front of him. He represented the various genuine activities and movements the Lord was directing in the Body of Christ throughout the world. He was resting his head in his hands because he was overwhelmed with the incredible volume of messages awaiting his reply.

I saw some of the names on the messages. Certain ones were from people interested in forming partnerships with the movements they believed God was emphasizing in this season of history; there was no guile in them. Other messages were from people who only wanted to be able to say that their personal ministries were connected with something God was legitimately doing. All they wanted was fame and recognition. The overwhelmed man asked, "How will I know whom to run with?"

I could see the Lord standing beside him with eyes like blazing fire, yet He answered with very simple, gentle statements.

"He who delights in the back of the line more than the front of the line.

"He who delights in being at the back table in the banquet room.

"He who finds delight in the lowest place."

Then the Lord said, "These are your comrades. These are the ones you will run with…and all the others will get pink slips."

Chapter 8

Saul of Tarsus

Prophetic dreams and prophetic words are invitations to join Jesus Christ, the Great Intercessor, in prayer for the purposes of God in the earth. When we join our prayers from all over the world with Jesus, change will come as He displays His power and saves to the uttermost (see Heb. 7:25).

I had a dream. I was standing in the "place of change" in Heaven. This place was like a council room. Decisions were made and requests were granted here because of the intercession that rises to the Lord.

As I stood on the floor, I saw golden lava bubbling and rising underneath me, and I knew it was an increase in intercession. The lava would rise through Heaven's floor, building up tension until it burst through the floor of the room to touch the Father's heart—and suddenly, the Son would decree *change*.

The scene changed and I was taken into an instance in history when intercession was at a high level. In my dream, I saw Saul (Paul) before and during his conversion. The dream was like watching a movie unfolding, particularly focusing on what was happening with Saul. I knew I was seeing the earthly result of heavenly change. Now Saul was consenting to Stephen's death:

> *Then Saul, still breathing threats and murder against the disciples of the Lord, went to the high priest and asked letters from him to the synagogues of Damascus, so that if he found any who were of the Way, whether men or women, he might bring them bound to Jerusalem. As he journeyed he came near Damascus, and suddenly a light shone around him from heaven. Then he fell to the ground, and heard a voice saying to him, "Saul, Saul, why are you persecuting Me?" And he said, "Who are You, Lord?" Then the Lord said, "I am Jesus, whom you are persecuting. It is hard for you to kick against the goads." So he, trembling and astonished, said, "Lord, what do You want me to do?" Then the Lord said to him, "Arise and go into the city, and you will be told what you must do"* (Acts 9:1-6).

I could see Saul, driven by perfectionist zeal, nodding his approval to Stephen's death with a little smirk on his face. I saw the bright light blazing all around as Saul fell to the ground. He fell hard too. I saw the story unfold line by line, like it was happening again.

Then a thunderous voice abruptly said, "It is going to happen again. There is a man who has set his heart against Me and My people Israel, but he is Mine. He is Mine. I am going to encounter him and turn his heart in one breath."

"And then...then...then...." The word *then* kept echoing and resounding through my head with a crescendo that grew increasingly sure.

"Then..." the voice said, "then Acts chapter 2 is going to happen all over again."

This dream came to me many times; and each time, Saul stood out to me. As the dream progressed, I saw the interaction between Saul and Ananias and how the Church did not believe Saul's conversion was genuine.

> *Now there was a certain disciple at Damascus named Ananias; and to him the Lord said in a vision, "Ananias." And he said, "Here I am, Lord." So the Lord said to him, "Arise and go to the street called Straight, and inquire at the house of Judas for one called Saul of Tarsus, for behold, he is praying. And in a vision he has seen a man named Ananias coming in and putting his hand on him, so that he might receive his sight." Then Ananias answered, "Lord, I have heard from many about this man, how much harm he has done to Your saints in Jerusalem. And here he has authority from the chief priests to bind all who call on Your name"* (Acts 9:10-14).

God did not show me who this modern-day Saul is, but I believe this person exists. In my dream, I remember thinking it was someone from the Middle East who is currently actively against God and Israel, a person who has a measure of authority or an amount of granted status.

In my dream, I saw the Lord bring this person into the Body of Christ, and it caused great controversy. But whenever and however this event happens, we are to know that the Lord is orchestrating this person's entire conversion. Until then, God has invited us to intercede until the Son decrees change.

Chapter 9

Becoming Fragrance

The Lord wants us to ask Him for more of His presence, His Spirit, and His gifts, yet often we are not ready for them, and we do not understand what we are praying for. The Lord wants to answer our prayers, but He must purify us first—and His refining of us comes from His passion for us. In His mercy and love, He brings many forms of pressure into our lives, watching to see what will arise from our hearts in response. Whether the scent is a fragrance depends on how we react when we understand that many times these pressures are His answer to our prayers. The process of crushing and refining is often painful and difficult, but if we respond in acceptance, we will be the sweet fragrance of prayer to Him.

I had a dream. In my dream, I woke up, got out of my bed, and walked to where an angel was standing at the foot of the bed. The angel was so brilliant that looking at him hurt my eyes. The angel said several times, "Pressure is coming. Pressure is coming."

I was shown a forge where silver is heated and purified by fire. I could feel the heat from the fire on my skin. Huge hands of a refiner were gently tending the silver in the extreme heat. I knew that the Refiner's hands were also the Potter's hands; the same hands that work the silver also mold the clay.

Suddenly, the scene changed and I was standing on the platform in a prayer room. In front of me was a huge boulder that had fallen through the roof. The Lord was standing beside the boulder, asking me, "Do you know what you ask for?" His voice was terrifying. It sounded like charging thunder, or like a huge wave about to crash down in the middle of a vast and resounding sea. He asked me again, "Do you know what you are asking for?" The power of His voice shook the whole room so much that I fell backward.

His eyes were like an inferno. As He looked around at the people in the prayer room, representing believers everywhere, He saw into the deepest parts of our beings and knew our hearts completely. I felt the terrifying tension of His eyes piercing us—seeing right through us and exposing every flaw and weakness—but simultaneously calling us to become who He intended us to be. I felt Him saying, "It's yours; just ask for it. I have been waiting since the foundations of the earth for people to cry out for it. I have been waiting to give it all. It's *yours*; just ask." I knew He was referring to the fullness of our destiny in Him, the gifts and relationship that have always been available to anyone who pursues Him. He wants us to ask for our inheritance in Him.

Again the scene changed, and I knew I would be experiencing something directed at all those in the Church who were crying out for more of God. I found myself at the foot of a large table as a shower of bread crumbs fell from this table onto the floor. I knew

I was in the parable of Matthew 15:25-28, in which Jesus tests the Canaanite woman's faith. I felt tremendous faith rise within me as I raced to grab each tumbling crumb. Jesus knew who He created His Church to be, but it is not enough for Jesus to say to us, "This is who you are." We have to believe it for ourselves. As I picked up the crumbs, I believed more and more in who Jesus said I was. Then the Lord said, "Woman, you have great faith."

I looked up and I could see the sky through the large hole in the roof. I saw a tremendous amount of brilliant white spots floating down toward the earth, so I thought it was snowing. But as the snow came nearer, I realized it was a throng of angels swarming by the hundreds into prayer rooms and churches across the world. This invasion of heavenly messengers and angelic activity steadily poured in through the open hole in the ceiling.

There were all kinds of angels with chariots and strong horses. Four mighty angels in chariots stationed themselves at all four corners of the building, standing guard over the people. They were warring angels and had a terrifying presence of authority.

Many of these brilliant messengers were dancing, some even in the air. Others had harps and were singing, "Hallelujah," and the sound of the music and the harmonies was like that of the largest, most entrancing choir I had ever heard. Some angels had paintbrushes and were painting bold colors on the ceiling, the walls, and in the air above people's heads.

Some angels had the sole mission of releasing the beauty of God. As they sang and danced, they scattered sparkling, tiny diamonds and sapphires all over the building. As the jewels came toward people, they became lodged in their inner selves—their souls, minds, and hearts. I saw gems planted in the area of the mind that receives understanding, while other gems came to rest in people's hearts. I reached up and caught one of the jewels. On it was written the word *understanding*. I reached up and caught another, which read *revelation*.

As these diamonds and sapphires were implanted, the people themselves began to shine with an inner glow, as if a great light had been turned on within them. The angels spun around in the air, loosing creativity and gifts of revelation; everything became imbued with vivid color, tangible beauty, and transcendent music. The music, the voices, and the sight of the angels eclipsed everything I have ever experienced in my life.

Suddenly, a mighty wind began to blow so hard that it knocked everyone to the ground. We were flat on the floor and could not get up—and it was amazing. All we could do was lie there and watch the angels continue in their activities. They rode the winds as they painted, sang, and released more revelation of God's beauty.

Then came an abrupt, heavy rain like nothing I have ever seen. It seemed as if a dam had broken in the heavens and the water would fill the building before we could react. We struggled to our feet. In what seemed like a blink of an eye, we were up to our waists in water. I remember thinking we did not even have time to get used to the water being at our ankles; the water level came right to our waists almost immediately. The angels kept doing their work, but we were not ready to receive what we had been asking for because the answer had come so fast. We were not prepared for such a quick response from Heaven. We were caught off guard by the outpouring of the Spirit.

The Potter and His Clay

The scene changed, and again I was standing at the foot of my bed watching the Lord tend the kiln with His huge hands. He intently watched the clay throughout every moment it took for the clay to be purified. There was such joy in the face of the Potter as He put pressure on the clay to make it into a beautiful sculpture. He had great joy in bringing pressure. He knew just what to do to make each part of the clay bend and fold. During this scene, I heard the angel say again, "Pressure is coming."

Refining is coming; the sculpting of an end-time people is coming. The sculpture has already been signed by the Great Potter Himself. He has marked His name on the clay.

I was shown the refining process from the perspective of Heaven, and I could see a vapor arising. As I looked down, I saw that it was coming from underneath the rock on the stage. The rising fragrance was like a valley full of wildflowers or a whole room filled with fresh roses. I looked up at the Lord. He was smiling as He said, "The unoffended prayers of the saints arise like sweet-smelling incense." Those who were not offended at God's refining process had offered up their prayers as a sweet fragrance that filled the corridors of Heaven.

I also saw black smoke arising that smelled like sulfur. The stench was produced by prayers that came from offense and anger. I realized that all prayers arise, and that the Lord really hears them all. How we live arises before the Lord either like a sweet fragrance or a sulfuric stench, depending upon our heart response to His refining and molding process.

I looked at the Lord, who was basking in the fragrance of the sweet perfume arising from the saints. He was smiling as if He was surrounded by the most beautiful fragrance in existence. I knew I was seeing Song of Solomon 1:12 play out in front of me: while the King is at His table, our perfume spreads its fragrance.

Suddenly I was back in my room again, still smelling that most beautiful fragrance of the unoffended prayers. I heard these words, "Remember this: the crushing brings about a fragrance that ascends to the throne. The pressure brings about a fragrance that ascends to the throne. The refining and molding brings about a fragrance that ascends to the throne. It all ascends; every part of how you live ascends."

Chapter 10

April Snow

The Father's kindness toward us is so good. In His mercy, He trains us to run the race of faith with excellence and wants us to give up everything that hinders us from running well. God rejoices when we tear our hearts in repentance and leave our sins behind (see Phil. 3:12-14). Repentance is an act of humility, love, and sacrifice, and it takes much humility to embrace righteousness. But if we will lean into our loving Father, He will give us grace as abundant as soaking rain.

I had a dream. This dream came the last week of February 2007, when the weather was unusually warm for Kansas City.

Many people were already wearing flip-flop sandals and shorts. It was so warm that I decided I should get my spring and summer clothes out.

In the dream, the Lord said, "Do not take out your spring and summer clothes yet, for there is still more snow coming—behold, even into April. With every snowflake that falls to the ground, I want you to remember righteousness, righteousness, righteousness. With every snowflake that falls to the ground, remember purity, purity, purity."

Then I was taken and placed in the middle of a large training area full of many people. This part of the dream was a picture of the Bride being prepared. We wore white jerseys, as if we were ready to compete in the Olympics, but we were not clean.

My eyes were opened to see writing on each jersey describing that person's secret life. I could see *selfish ambition* written on some jerseys. I saw *gossip* on others. I saw *grumbling* and *complaining*—these sins were highlighted as big deals to God. Some people's jerseys were labeled with sexual sins: *lustful thoughts, pornography, adultery,* and *fornication.* God was watching every hidden thing. Despite the secrets we kept to ourselves in darkness, He saw everything.

> *...Even the night shall be light about me; indeed, the darkness shall not hide from You, but the night shines as the day; the darkness and the light are both alike to You* (Psalm 139:11-12).

The Lord appeared with a dual expression of His heart in the dream. He was at once the tender Father and the firm athletic Coach. He had so much passion for us to become the greatest that He created us to be. He was training us because He was determined that we would win the race.

> *Not that I have already attained, or am already perfected; but I press on, that I may lay hold of that for which Christ Jesus has also laid hold of me. Brethren, I do not count myself to have apprehended; but*

one thing I do, forgetting those things which are behind and reaching forward to those things which are ahead, I press toward the goal for the prize of the upward call of God in Christ Jesus (Philippians 3:12-14).

The Lord looked at us in our soiled jerseys with desire and determination. He was desirous of our affection and of our maturity, and He was determined about our future with Him. As a Father, He was full of love for us even in our weakness, but He did not want us to stay weak. He wanted us in the race. He was overjoyed with our choice to follow Him, even though He knew there was much work to be done.

I could feel His fatherly heart and how He longed to take care of us. At the same time, His eyes were focused like a training coach. He was intent on preparing us. He cautioned us, saying, "You are not yet ready." And He intended to get us ready.

He showed me that there would be a season of intense rain in addition to the season of snow in Kansas City. I saw the rain saturate the ground. The Lord kept saying, "With every drop of rain that falls to the ground, I am sending grace upon grace to get you free from that which trips you up, from the sin that so easily entangles you. Remember grace."

The Scripture highlighted to me was Hosea 6:1 and 3: *"Come, and let us return to the LORD...He will come to us like the rain...."*

The scene changed, and I saw people standing in a line, waiting to pray publicly. One by one, they stepped forward and prayed the same thing from Isaiah 64:1: *"Oh* [Lord], *that You would rend the heavens! That You would come down!"*

Stationed in between each person were enormous angels. The angels responded to each prayer with a cry more intense and powerful than the cry of any person in the prayer line. With the Word of God already open in their hands, the angels responded with Joel

2:13 to each prayer. They cried with a voice like the sea, "You rend *your* heart."

Each intercessor in the line would open his or her Bible and pray. The angel behind the intercessor would respond immediately, and then another intercessor would follow.

"God, rend the heavens."

"You rend *your* heart."

"God, rend the heavens."

"You rend *your* heart."

I watched this back-and-forth interaction for a while. The compassionate, steady gaze of the Father was upon us, the One who was training us and who wanted to purify us. His gaze was so kind and tender. His eyes danced with pure enjoyment as the intercessors prayed. He breathed in the prayers, taking in the fragrance that arose to Him.

He said, "I am sending signs to let you know I am coming to help you. The snow is coming as a reminder of righteousness. The rain is coming as My promise to move the heavenly hosts on your behalf, because I want a pure and shining Bride. If you will do your part, I am going to come along behind you and shove you into victory. When you see the snow, think of Me. When you see the rain, think of Me."

I asked the Lord, "How do I do this? How do I live holy?"

He answered, "You do not have to climb the mountain of holiness and perfection in one day. Do it this way: day by day, step by step, choice by choice, and yes by yes. It is one day at a time, one step at a time, one choice at a time, and one yes at a time. You may not be perfect for the rest of the week, but your next choice can be a yes for Me, and your next choice after that. If you mess up, press delete, and quickly get right back into step.

"If you will do the little thing of taking the step-by-step journey, then I will do the big thing and set you free. That which tripped you up yesterday is what you will tread upon tomorrow."

As we ran the race, the wind of God's grace came behind each person and shoved us through the finish line. Each person individually broke the ribbon at the end of the race. All the sin written on each jersey fell off, and the jerseys transformed into pristine white.

After weeks of unusually warm weather, the April snow came on Friday, April 13. It began at 8:00 P.M. and continued until 6:00 A.M. on April 14. The unprecedented rains started around 11:00 P.M. on May 5 and continued for over two days. The nearby Blue River spilled over its banks on the last day of the rain.[1]

ENDNOTE

1. To view precipitation reports for Missouri, go to http://water.weather.gov.

Chapter 11

Banquet Table

The overall shout of joy in this dream comes from Song of Solomon 5:1, when the Lord says to believers, "...Eat, O friends! Drink, yes, drink deeply, O beloved ones!" God's passion and love for us are deeper than the deepest ocean, and His gifts are innumerable. We could spend our entire lives trying to search out and understand the joy and affection that Jesus Christ has for us, and still we would only touch the mere edges of His great passion. The limitless feast He offers us is Himself: everyone is invited to partake of the knowledge of God and the love He has for us, expressed through His Word and Spirit. I love this dream because it showed me that even as He guides our lives and disciplines us, He has great joy in helping us become all that He created us to be.

I had a dream. I was invited to a banquet given by the Lord. All of the Church was invited to this banquet. It was outside in the middle of a wide, green pasture under a vivid blue sky. The tables were arranged in rows and each table was covered with a red-and-white checkered tablecloth. On the tables, the Lord had placed large, brown baskets filled with the most colorful fruit for us to eat. I could look at the colors of the fruit and almost taste it in my mouth. The fruit was so beautiful and inviting; just the sight of it drew my heart to the Lord and made my mouth water and tingle.

The fruit represented the knowledge of God and intimacy with Him—knowing His heart, His emotions, and His great love for us. He wanted us to eat this fruit and to feed on Him. I understood that I was looking at a picture of Song of Solomon 2:3-4, *"...I sat down in his shade with great delight, and his fruit was sweet to my taste. He brought me to the banqueting house, and his banner over me was love."*

Jesus was so happy that we were eating the fruit. He would walk from table to table, enjoying watching people eat. The more everyone ate, the more He would laugh and say, "The fruit is for everyone. Eat, My friends!" His laugh and His joy were unrestrained. I had never imagined how much joy Jesus Christ has. Psalm 45:7 says He is the most joyful Man to have walked this earth; He is anointed with gladness.

Jesus wanted everyone to partake of His feast. The people responded in various ways. All around me I saw different people, each representing a different facet of the Church, feasting on what Jesus was offering. One group was diving in and eating the fruit because they were leaders. They knew they were responsible for feeding themselves because they needed to feed and lead the people.

Then there were the people who were not leaders. Many of them just looked at the fruit and watched the leaders eat, but did not taste of it themselves. The Lord said, "It is for everyone. The fruit is for all of you. Everyone, eat." But they only looked at the food without touching it. Some did not feel worthy enough to eat. They did not believe the invitation was truly for them.

It's Our Decision

I realized that all people have a choice of whether they accept the Lord's invitation or just observe others. All those who only watched and would not partake of the feast eventually ended up leaving the banquet. Although they were still saved, they did not experience the joy of deeper intimacy with God or receive all of the riches He wanted to give them. They heard the invitation to pursue more of God, but chose to pursue something else.

When I saw this, it provoked me to dive in and eat as much fruit as possible from the Lord's table. I didn't want to sit and watch other people eat; I wanted to feast on the fruit for myself. In the dream I ate so much that my cheeks hurt.

I saw a woman who represented worship leaders in the Church putting fruit in her backpack. She kept her backpack full of fruit and ate it all day long as she walked around. She was carrying so much fruit that it was falling out. Young girls were picking up and eating the dropped fruit. They were learning from the woman to feast on the Lord, guiding them to look to God for their own fruit.

Two people who represented children's ministry were tossing fruit up in the air for children around them to catch in their mouths. The two ministers were acting out Matthew 19:14, *"But*

Jesus said, 'Let the little children come to Me, and do not forbid them; for of such is the kingdom of heaven.'"

I saw two people who represented the prophetic ministry in the Church. The Lord stood behind them and said, "They always give away twice as much fruit as they eat because they want everyone to taste of the sweetness of Christ and the sweetness of prophecy. I see all that they do in secret."

THIS IS FOR EVERYONE

One man who represented the gifts of prophecy and tongues was eating and speaking in tongues. The Lord stood behind him and said, "There is a reservoir of prophetic declarations and prophetic words that the Lord is getting ready to spill out from you. You will be like a volcano, exploding with the prophetic word of God from the inside. The word will be like lava, setting on fire all who hear it and burning the dross away."

I saw a Southern gentleman who represented the healing ministry. The Lord called him "the one who rallies." He was encouraging everyone just like Jesus was doing. He was eating so much, laughing, and yelling at everyone, "He is really, really serious, y'all! You must eat. He really wants us to eat!" As he talked, food was flying out of his mouth everywhere and hitting people. He just kept eating and saying, "He is really serious. Jesus is really serious. This is for everyone." Another man and woman from the healing ministry were feeding people who were lame, blind, or deaf and could not feed themselves. They were taking fruit and putting it into the mouths of the outcasts.

A man who ministered to the lost was backing up a truck to the tables. He got out and said, "Load 'em up." He was taking the fruit to the highways and byways and telling people about the sweetness of the fruit. Another evangelist took a huge basket of fruit and went into a meadow filled with flowers. He ran through the field, laughing with joy and tossing fruit into the air. The flowers, which represented people, opened their mouths and ate the fruit.

I saw a man seated at the table eating and typing, feeding himself and others through the message he was writing.

I saw a woman who represented believers working in the marketplace. When she ate the fruit, her whole countenance became colorful like the fruit. It was as if she *became* color. The marketplace Christians whom she led took the fragrance of this fruit everywhere, even when they did not realize it, and by doing so led people to the Lord.

I saw two men who were like John the apostle, the disciple whom Jesus loved. They were spiritual fathers with tender hearts like the Shepherd (see Ps. 23:1). They were eating the fruit and enjoying watching everyone feast on the banquet. They leaned into Jesus just as John did, then went to the tables of the people who were not eating and lovingly encouraged them to take that first bite.

I saw many other leaders who were spiritual mothers and fathers. The Lord said they were the shepherds of people's hearts, and a new understanding of things to come—an understanding of John 19:25-27 and Revelation 4:1—would be coming to them.

Many youth were eating the fruit and laughing and throwing it at each other. They were saying to each other, "The fruit is my message." They were part of a whole group that the Lord called "The Young, Dreaded Champions." I saw many of its leaders throwing fruit to this army of young men and women of valor. One young leader was singing a new anthem, drawing a new generation of young adults—people of different cultures and races—into a deeper understanding of the love of Christ.

A young female leader was throwing fruit to the young people. In all boldness and confidence, she was charging them, "Prophesy!" The Lord stood behind her and said, "You are not only beautiful on the outside, you are beautiful on the inside; your humility is your greatest beauty." She was beautiful because of the great amount of humility she had cultivated.

One man who represented believers who had gone through the dark night of the soul—a time of spiritual pain that eventually leads to greater intimacy with God—was eating with great thankfulness. He was glad to taste the Lord's fruit again. He had tears rolling down his face and he kept saying, "You are so good to me, God. You are so good to me."

I saw a woman who led a dance ministry leading the dancers at her table. They would eat and then they would dance the colors of the fruit. It was not just a dance; it was warfare and prophecy.

I saw a whole section of people eating in the dark. They represented those who stand by night in the sanctuary of the Lord, praying and worshiping. They were laughing, they were loud, and they were really a family. The Lord went over to them and said, "Watch this." He snapped His fingers and a glowing, brilliant light appeared in their midst. He said, "The people singing through the darkness will see the Great Light."

The Place of Humility

As I looked around at those who were feasting at the table, I saw that some liked the place of honor. They liked to sit with the leaders and eat at their table. The Lord invited these people who loved the place of honor to go to a table near the back of the feast. He took them by the hand with great joy and excitedly said, "You get to sit here with just Me and the fruit until you love this place." He did not say, "You *have* to sit here in the place of humility," but said, "You *get* to sit here." He invited them into His great plans of delight and joy even amid discipline.

Other people who were already sitting in places of humility were also going to experience a change in position. The amount of favor the Lord showed them was stunning. He promoted them to places of honor at the feast because their only agenda was to love God, to know Him, and to seek Him out.

Jesus had great affection for those who found delight in being in the back of the room. I saw two worship leaders. One was sitting alone at a table, just eating, and the Lord took his table and shoved it to the front. It happened so fast that he had to hang on with all of his strength to stay at the table. Then the Lord took the table of fruit the man was sitting at and threw it like a Frisbee right through the sky. He was giving the man a highly visible position, sending his songs out to the nations to give them fruit. The other worship leader was hidden. Jesus told her, "You will surprise everyone and bless the nations with your songs."

As I looked around at the different people and watched them enjoy the feast, I understood that the Lord really wants us to delight in His banquet table. No matter who we are, we can know that He loves it when we enjoy His affections and taste of His fruit (see Song of Sol. 2:3-4).

The fruit is every facet, characteristic, and attribute of Jesus Christ as displayed in the Word of God. To feast on each Scripture in the Bible is to feast on the Lord. He invites everyone to eat and drink their fill, to taste and see that He is good.

Chapter 12

What Goes Up

I had this next dream on July 5, 2004. I shared it with many people who understand the stock market, but each one told me it would never happen. "The stock of pancakes will never soar," they said. "It will never shoot through the roof. If it were technology, computers, or oil, the stock would have potential to soar, but never pancakes; pancakes don't have that kind of potential." I refused to be deterred. I kept asking for an open heaven.

On July 17, 2007, the front page of USA Today read, "Stock of International House of Pancakes Soars."[1] The International House of Pancakes bought out Applebee's International, and the stock of pancakes rose dramatically (9 percent gain), just like the dream I had three years prior.

I had a dream. I was sitting at the International House of Prayer–Kansas City when I saw a white, glowing angel approach me and whisper in my ear, "When the stock of the International House of Pancakes shoots through the roof, be watchful; look up." I knew the stock of IHOP pancakes would be a sign that help was coming (see Ps. 121:1-2). The angel continued, "As the prayers of the saints ascend, what goes up must come down. As the prayers of the saints ascend, what goes up must come down." The angel repeated this over and over.

Wham! Out of nowhere, a 5-by-5-foot boulder fell through the roof right onto the platform. Everyone in the prayer room looked at the massive rock and the enormous hole it had made in the ceiling. In fact, there was no ceiling anymore. We sat in stunned silence, looking up at the sky.

I remember pinching myself, saying, "I can feel my skin, so I must be awake." But the angel ignored my rambling and kept whispering, "As the prayers of the saints ascend, what goes up must come down. As the prayers of the saints ascend, what goes up must come down."

Another angel with great authority took me to see a man who was praying and studying his Bible, focusing on Daniel, Zechariah, and Revelation. This man represented all who are willing to pursue revelation of the end times, those who are fully devoted to waiting on the Lord.

The angel said, "They have been asking for understanding to a mystery in Revelation. After a season, those devoted to God will be presented with a golden key of needed truth." I saw a long, golden key made for opening lockboxes. I knew this key was not general understanding or a word of knowledge, but revelation about the end times in particular. This key is not just for one person; it is for all who are willing. I knew the Lord desired that His people would have deep understanding of the end times, and that Daniel 12:4 and 9 should be relayed to them unto that end—for it is time to seek more understanding of the end times.

ENDNOTE

I. Several sources offer more information about the results of this transaction:

A. Evelyn M. Rusli, "IHOP Bites Into Applebees," *Forbes* online edition. http://www.forbes.com/markets/2007/07/16/ihop-applebees-dining-markets-equity-cx_er_0716markets09.html (accessed November 5, 2010).

B. IHOP stock jumps on $2.1B Applebee's bid," CNN Money.com. http://money.cnn.com/2007/07/16/news/companies/ihop_applebees/index.htm (accessed November 5, 2010).

C. Vinnee Tong, "IHOP to buy Applebee's for about $1.9B," *USA Today* online edition. The article states, "Under the deal, IHOP will pay $25.50 per share for Applebee's, a 4.6 percent premium over its closing price on Friday. Applebee's shares rose 53 cents, or 2.2 percent, to $24.91 in trading Monday. In an unusual move for the shares of a buyer, IHOP stock gained even more, rising $4.99, or 8.9 percent, to $61.24 after briefly reaching a new 52-week high of $63.39." http://www.usatoday.com/money/economy/2007-07-16-4078831354_x.htm (accessed November 5, 2010).

Chapter 13

Kings and Princes

I believe we are to pray for England, asking God to bring light to the hearts of kings and princes, and to encourage houses of prayer, especially the small groups of faithful people meeting in homes. This will bring about the plan of the Lord for that nation (see I Tim. 2:1-3).

I had a dream. It was like I was watching a movie about future events in England. I saw the Lord begin to stir a great number of women and men across England to pray. Small groups, sometimes only three to ten people, met in homes together to intercede for their land and to ask the Lord to raise up righteous leaders. I saw houses of prayer raised up one by one across the nation. Because of this prayer movement, rays of light started breaking through the dark cloud that had shrouded the nation. I saw that as the people prayed and as houses of prayer began to arise all over the land, God brought light to the hearts of the kings and princes. The prayers of the saints arose to Heaven and light broke forth on earth—for what goes up must come down.

THE SECOND BORN

In this dream, the Lord made a declaration: "I have not forgotten you, England. I have not forgotten you. There is a young royal who has made headlines from nation to nation. But I will take his wildness and turn it for good. I will encounter him who is red and ruddy, the second born of his father. He will walk alongside his brother, like Nathan the prophet walked alongside King David. You call him Harry, I call him Jacob. Together, the one like King David and the one like Jacob will lead a cry for righteousness in the land. This wave of righteousness will be as a tidal wave, reaching even Australia—and when England reaches out its hands to Australia, they will accept the invitation."

God was making it known that He has chosen leaders like King David—those who have hearts after God (see Acts 13:22). I saw the Lord begin to shed light on the true motives of the leaders of the land; little by little, their hearts were exposed. I saw that the Lord had already been visiting the Queen of England in dreams. The Lord said, "A great controversy will arise in England as I bring light to the hearts and motives of the kings and princes. A great cry for righteousness shall arise from the people in the land." The prayers of individuals, small groups, and houses of prayer are highly esteemed by God. As citizens begin to pray and houses of prayer arise, the Lord's will for the land and its leaders will be done in that nation.

The Lord saw some of the leaders of the land walk up the steps to a mosque, which was called the "House of Allah" in my dream, and declare their allegiance to a foreign god. They vowed to embrace all religions for the sake of humanity, pledging their allegiance in return for great favor and fame.

The Lord saw and heard those leaders say, "My leadership is inevitable. Even God Himself could not change my position." At that point, I saw the Lord's hand holding a stamp. He stamped the word *rejected* in big, bold, red letters across the papers of those leaders. God was making it known that He has instead chosen leaders like King David—those who have hearts after God (see Acts 13:22).

I saw the Lord begin to shed light on the true motives of the leaders of the land; little by little, their hearts were exposed. I saw that the Lord had already been visiting the Queen of England in dreams.

The Lord said, "A great controversy will arise in England as I bring light to the hearts and motives of the kings and princes. A great cry for righteousness shall arise from the people in the land."

The prayers of individuals, small groups, and houses of prayer are highly esteemed by God. As citizens begin to pray and houses of prayer arise, the Lord's will for the land and its leaders will be done in that nation.

Chapter 14

Out of America's East

Satan intends to increase the spirit of witchcraft across America—starting many fires, stirring up smoke, and spreading fear. This spirit of witchcraft, which will be released like nothing our nation has yet seen, is going to be lies from hell: persuasive and deceptive. The enemy will lure many to bow to him out of fear instead of bowing to God in faith with prayer and intimacy. But there is one way to fight it and to encounter the Lord in the midst of the shaking: go low—pray. This is the place where we must live.

I had a dream. I saw a strong spirit of witchcraft come from America's East. It was released through key people in governmental places, including women. Everything coming from the mouth of this spirit is not truth and not the word of the Lord. His heart and His plans are not to be found in the message.

The enemy wants to lure the Church out of its place of power, which is on its knees. The Church must go low in faith and intimacy with God.

In my dream, I had to push my head down to the ground and tell myself, "Go low. Pray." From this position, I could tell the coming battle—the struggle to go low, to pray, and to embrace humility—would be hard, very hard.

"Go Low. Pray."

Lies stir up fear in the heart. Many Christian leaders will try to fight this battle with words, but they will only add to the fear, confusion, and havoc being released.

The Lord is inviting us to go low with Him. Going low is the place of encountering God, so it is the place of power and change. If the Church will go low in prayer, we will emerge unwavering in our faith, we will be untouched by the enemy's lies, and we will encounter the Lord in the midst of the havoc felt across the nation.

The Church is not just those who sit in sanctuaries on Sunday mornings, but those who pray, those who go low when the land is in crisis. This is His description of the Church from Second Chronicles 7:13-18:

> When I shut up heaven and there is no rain, or command the locusts to devour the land, or send pestilence among My people, if My people who are called by My name will humble themselves, and pray and seek My face, and turn from their wicked ways, then I will hear from heaven, and will forgive their sin and heal their land. Now My eyes will be open and My ears attentive to prayer made in this place. For now I have chosen and sanctified this house, that My name may

be there forever; and My eyes and My heart will be there perpetually.
As for you, if you walk before Me as your father David walked,
and do according to all that I have commanded you, and if you keep
My statutes and My judgments, then I will establish the throne of
your kingdom, as I covenanted with David your father, saying,
"You shall not fail to have a man as ruler in Israel."

God has raised up many houses of prayer and many expres-
sions of the prayer movement around the world for such a time as
this. Yes, the prayer movement will start small, but it will end up
as an army of voices who are established in the place of intimacy—
those who are on their knees with a thriving faith, crying out to
the God who answers prayer.

Chapter 15

New York City: The City of Great Lights

When we look at New York City, we often do not look past the financial power of Wall Street, the glitter of Broadway, and the height of worldly markets and industries. We do not see how the people are trapped in the city's spiritual darkness. But God looks at New York and calls its people out into a greater destiny of prayer and of knowing Him, "The people who walked in darkness have seen a great light; those who dwelt in the land of the shadow of death, upon them a light has shined" (Isa. 9:2).

I had a dream. I was looking down on New York City from above. It was night, and I could see the lights of the city shining through the darkness.

The Lord said, "New York, you have been a prisoner to your own darkness, but I call you the City of Great Lights. I call you a city that is set on a hill and the salt of the earth. Therefore, to you who fear My name, on the very corner where the door of devastation was opened, the Son of Righteousness shall arise with healing in His wings" (see Mal. 4:2).

"I will spread My wings far and wide and from one edge of the city to the other, you will be covered with healing. At the place where devastation occurred, salvation, righteousness, healing, and revival will spring up. I will raise up the tabernacle of David, which has fallen down, and repair its damages; I will raise up its ruins, and rebuild it as in the days of old" (see Amos 9:11).

I could see that the Lord already had a space reserved for His house of prayer to overlook the City of Great Lights. The Lord is stirring up His watchmen so that day-and-night prayer will go out and rest as a mist over the city.

I saw the Lord focus on Broadway. He had a plan to impact creativity and the arts. A Broadway musical will spring up in the heart of New York with a name like *Out of Egypt*. The Lord will arise and come to the Jewish community and the people living in an area He called the Northeastern Gate. He will reveal Himself as the God of Israel and His Son Yeshua as Messiah.

The musical run will start with a man named Tony and will end with a statuette named Tony. The angels themselves will make the curtain calls. In my dream, I felt that the angels may appear during or at the end of the musical, and the natural eye may be able to see them.

At the end of its run, this musical will cross the waters of the great deep and land within the walls of Jerusalem with new music and new sounds. It will once again introduce the people of Israel to the Lord God of Israel and to Yeshua the Messiah. The angels will again appear. When this musical lands in Jerusalem, it will crush the idols of Kabbalah.

Chapter 16

The Key of Intercession

This dream is a call to prayer. As the nations of the earth begin to pray, breakthrough will happen in many nations. The key is simultaneous intercession in many lands, accompanied by humility. God promises to hear our prayers and heal our land when we seek His face and turn from sin.

I had a dream. The Lord handed a key to intercessors across the nations. The key separated into three unique pieces but became perfectly entwined, sealed, and unbreakable when put together. It was the key of intercession. He gave it to the three nations that—without intercessors—were not likely to come together in unity: the United States, England, and Korea.

Written on the back of the key was Second Chronicles 7:14:

If My people who are called by My name will humble themselves, and pray and seek My face, and turn from their wicked ways, then I will hear from heaven, and will forgive their sin and heal their land.

The Spirit of the Lord spoke three words to me and then paused to brand them on my heart: "If My people." He wanted me to understand that it was a conditional invitation.

In this dream, I was taken back into two prior dreams I had experienced and then shown the third part, as if to see how they interacted with one another. First, the Lord brought me back to a dream that dealt with America. He had said in that dream: "If My people who have been given the key will pray for that which I am doing, a visitation will come to the highest office of the United States of America. I will turn the president's heart straight into My purposes like a river" (see Prov. 21:1). "I am going to do what man said could not be done. I am going to supersede that which man says is law. Watch and pray."

The Lord also said, "If My people who have been given the key will pray for that which I am doing, then I will also visit England." He took me back to the dream of England's kings and princes, in which He had said: "I have not forgotten you, England. I have not forgotten you. There is a young royal who has made headlines from nation to nation. But I will take his wildness and turn it for good. I will encounter him who is red and ruddy, the second born of his father. He will walk alongside his brother like Nathan the prophet walked alongside King David. Though you call him Harry, I call him Jacob, and he will lead a great Jacob generation.

The Spirit of the Lord said, "I will encounter the second born first and He shall lead a cry for righteousness in England. My eyes are on one like Jacob and on one like King David. Together they will intercede for righteousness in the land. Though a cloud arises over the land, a great light shall blaze out of it."

KOREA

The scene changed. I was shown the continuation of the first and second dreams. I saw great fear arising in Korea: murmurings and whispers of those planning evil, darkness, and great destruction. The Lord said, "If My people who have been given the key will pray for that which I am doing, then I will also visit So Korea."

In my dream I saw that, even as talk of a nuclear bomb spreads throughout the nations like wildfire, something greater than a nuclear bomb will explode out of Korea—the Son of Righteousness will arise with healing in His wings. As the Lord's people humble themselves and pray, Korea will be refined in the fire and washed white as snow (see Mal. 3:2-3). God will break down the wall between generations; He will turn the hearts of the fathers toward the children and the hearts of the children to the fathers (see Mal. 4:6).

As generational reconciliation happens, an unstoppable wave of intercession will spring up from within Korea like a tsunami and will touch many nations, reaching even to the borders of Israel. Yet this wave will not tear down. It will build up and heal. As Koreans pray, they will be made ready for a great move of the Spirit.

Then, with great weight, the Spirit of the Lord said, "Watch for the signs. He who has ears to hear, let him hear. Watch for a brand-new bloom in the desert. Watch for a brand-new color in the sky. Watch for a tsunami of intercession to spring up from within Korea, for this great wave will touch the ends of the earth, even into Israel—if My people will pray."

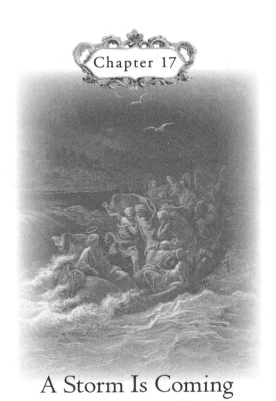

Chapter 17

A Storm Is Coming

The sons of Issachar knew the signs of the times and what to do (see 1 Chron. 12:32). Whenever we see signs, we need to ask God what He is saying so that we can interpret them correctly and not become caught up with the signs themselves.

I had a dream. I was at a gathering that felt like a big family celebration. My children were there, and others had brought their children as well. Most of the people attending served in positions of leadership: worship leaders and team members, small-group leaders, teachers, and the like.

All of a sudden, a gentle breeze began to blow and got increasingly stronger. There was a huge 5-by-5-foot picture window that rattled as the wind intensified. The rattling got my attention and, as I looked around the room, I noticed that others were also beginning to pay attention.

I looked out through the window and saw that new colors had overtaken the sky. Instead of white clouds, I saw large crimson clouds and bright green clouds. They were tumbling and billowing and burning brightly. It was startling.

Then I looked, and behold, a whirlwind was coming out of the north, a great cloud with raging fire engulfing itself; and brightness was all around it and radiating out of its midst like the color of amber, out of the midst of the fire (Ezekiel 1:4).

We were awestruck by the breathtaking beauty of the contrasting colors. We stood in silence, marveling at the clouds and wondering what this sight could mean. After a few moments, each person began quoting various Scriptures as they strained to give meaning to the sign.

"The heavens declare the glory of God…The Son is the radiance of God's glory…The grace of God that brings salvation has appeared to all men…The righteousness of God extends to the clouds…Do not put out the Spirit's fire…Jesus Christ will be glorified in His holy people and marveled at by all those who have believed."

Though each Scripture was a true statement, God was saying something different. Those watching were so caught up in the sign itself that they missed its true meaning: a storm was coming. Fearful dread—the raw fear of the Lord—suddenly gripped me because I knew none of them had interpreted the sign correctly.

THERE IS A STORM COMING

Next to me stood a man who was like a son of Issachar. He was seasoned in leadership and had great prophetic understanding because of his many years spent at the Lord's feet. He shook his head as if to say of the verses everyone had mentioned, "No, those are not the correct interpretation." In a measured, slow whisper of certainty and sobriety, he explained the sign clearly: "There is a storm coming. There is a storm coming, Beloved. There is a storm coming."

Signs are meant to direct us into dialogue with God; they are not an end in themselves. We must look past signs, no matter how great or terrifying they seem, and ask the Lord for the right interpretation.

This is the time we get to actually talk to God and ask Him, "What are You doing? What do these signs mean? What is on Your heart? Tell me, God, what You are wanting me to know." Then we simply listen to the Spirit of the Lord on the inside and begin to pray out of what we are hearing. The Spirit of the Lord is the greatest Teacher. He will guide us and reveal to us what is on the heart of the Father (see 1 Cor 2:9-10).

That is when we become a voice and correctly understand what God is doing in our times and seasons and proclaim it. We become like the sons of Issachar in First Chronicles 12:32 who had understanding of the times, to know what Israel ought to do. The Spirit of the Lord will train us in the same way so that we also know the signs of the times and what we must do.

Turning Hearts

God is inviting the elder generation——from the parents to the great-grandparents——to come out of retirement. It is not time to retire; it is time to re-fire. He has prepared a place for you as a pillar in a prayer and worship movement that will change the face of Christianity and will last until the return of Jesus Christ. He is turning the hearts of the fathers and the children toward each other. Come, for the young generation is in need of you.

I had a dream. It was from Malachi 4:5-6:

Behold, I will send you Elijah the prophet before the coming of the great and dreadful day of the LORD. And he will turn the hearts

*of the fathers to the children, and the hearts of the children to their
fathers, lest I come and strike the earth with a curse.*

I saw a water pitcher made from clear glass. But this pitcher
had only one side, as if someone had cut it from top to bottom. I
knew if anything was poured into the pitcher, it would run right
out because the container was incomplete.

I saw it sitting on a table. The pitcher could stand on its own
as long as everything was completely still, but it would fall over if
any kind of shaking or vibration disturbed it. It was not balanced
since it had only one side.

I heard the Lord say, "This glass pitcher represents the hearts
of both the younger and older generations. It is incomplete, but I
am going to make it completely whole. I am turning the hearts of
the children and the fathers toward each other. Both sides of the
pitcher must be set in place to receive the outpouring of My Spirit
and to be able to stand in the midst of the shaking."

I saw the following Scripture play out in front of my eyes:

Elisha had [previously] *become sick with the illness of which he
would die. Then Joash the king of Israel came down to him, and
wept over his face, and said, "O my father, my father, the chariots of
Israel and their horsemen!" And Elisha said to him, "Take a bow and
some arrows." So he took himself a bow and some arrows. Then he
said to the king of Israel, "Put your hand on the bow." So he put his
hand on it, and Elisha put his hands on the king's hands* (2 Kings
13:14-16).

I knew Elisha represented the older generation while the king
was the younger generation. In my dream, when Elisha put his
hands on the king's hands, I saw the king shrug off Elisha. It was as
if the younger generation believed they did not need the influence
or guidance of the prior generation.

The Lord said, "I am going to change this because I want a movement that will last until My return. The dads, moms, grandfathers, and grandmothers must be in place as pillars of the movement so it will not burn out."

The older generation represents longevity and faithfulness in the Lord through good times and dark times, through seasons of favor and seasons of demotion. The younger generation represents the youth revival that will sweep through the nations of the earth.

Then the Lord said three things:

"Healing is coming to moms and dads, grandmothers and grandfathers who feel disqualified by their pasts, but their pasts are the very reason they are qualified. Come again and find your place on the wall. This generation of youth is in need of you.

"Healing is coming to the hearts of children who come from abused backgrounds. Where the older generation has brought them pain, they do not want to open their hearts to them. So I am going to set new spiritual moms and dads in their lives to bring them healing, and their hearts will be softened.

"I will crush the spirit of elitism between the generations, the spirit that puffs up. I will turn hearts so that love is the seal uniting both generations. The youth will run and soar like eagles, and the older generation will stand as pillars in a movement that will last until Jesus Christ returns."

Chapter 19

Time to Dance

The Lord is giving us a great invitation to lift our voices, to join the Great Intercessor and pray for His friends: for the poor, for the unborn, and for the apple of His eye, Israel. Prayer connects us to God's heart; our hearts are united with His. We begin to feel the depths of His passion for those who seemingly have no voice. When we begin to understand His emotions about the injustice on the earth, we will enter into a new kind of intercession.

I had a dream. The Lord came to me and said, "I want you to meet My friends." I was excited because I thought I was going to meet Isaiah, Peter, or Moses. He took me by the hand and we flew loop-de-loops through the sky like we were in a cartoon. Even though we were extremely high above the ground, I was aware of not being afraid; I loved just holding His hand and feeling the wind on my face.

Suddenly His countenance changed. He set His face intently toward earth and we started heading directly toward the ground in a head-first dive. I thought, *Surely we aren't going to hit the ground.* But when I looked at His face, I could see fierce determination in His eyes.

> ...*Therefore I have set My face like a flint, and I know that I will not be ashamed* (Isaiah 50:7).

I knew He had already decided what He was going to do. He was not going to turn around. I felt horrible dread come over me as we kept descending, even though I was holding His hand.

We didn't crash. We exploded right through the ground like a scene from an action movie. I could see the impact as we blasted through the ground. I could hear the earth exploding around us as we traveled through rock, water, and burning fire. The sound was deafening, like the sound of a rocket being launched. I felt the earth pounding my head and rattling my body, and I could feel my skin burning and tearing. I was in immense pain in my dream, yet the Lord's face never turned to the left or right; His eyes were fixed straight ahead.

Suddenly we burst through the other side of the earth. I stood there looking at my body for a moment, in shock at what had just happened. My skin was lacerated. My body was weak and aching. I was crying because I was in so much pain. I thought, *Surely He sees how badly I am hurt and how badly my skin is wounded and torn.* Jesus was aware of my pain, but He made it known that it was not about me. He said to me, "I want you to meet My friends."

He began walking. As I followed Him, I noticed that we were in a very crowded place. I knew it was a city in India. There were young, suffering children everywhere. I saw some lying on the ground with flies crawling on their skin. As they passed from their horrible circumstances into the next life, He was there for each one the moment they awakened in eternity. I saw beautiful young girls in cages, with whom He continually stood. The Lord calls these seemingly forgotten ones His friends. Not one of them is forgotten in His eyes.

MY FRIENDS

The sadness of what I was seeing, along with the agonizing pain my body felt, left me in tears. The Lord came over to look me in the eye. I thought He had finally noticed my pain and was coming to comfort me. Instead, He revealed my self-centered response and invited me to feel His heart: "Until your heart is torn like your flesh is now, you do not know how I feel about My friends."

He wanted me to feel the pain of the cuts in my skin so I could understand how His heart is torn. I saw children dying, mothers taking their last breath, young girls being sold, and disease spreading. It was more than I could handle. He said again, "Until your heart is torn like your flesh is now, you do not know how I feel about My friends. You do not know Me."

As I looked at the staggering injustice all around, to my surprise, He came near me to reveal His secret weapon against it. He whispered, "It is time to dance."

He began a rhythmic, tribal stomp. His perfect feet with their scars of passion were bringing justice by stomping out the injustice done to His friends. He said again, "Until your heart is torn in two, you do not know how I feel about My friends. You do not know Me."

Then He grabbed my hand and we blasted through the center of the earth again. I could feel the horrible pain of my flesh tearing away from my bones and hear the thunderous sound as we pushed through layers of earth. When we came out on the other side, we were in some kind of clinic that was cold, bleak, and unfeeling. My first thought was of myself and how much pain I was in. I felt as if I had no skin on my bones, like it had all been ripped off. Through my pain, I could hear Jesus say to me again, "I want you to meet My friends."

I looked around and saw trashcans filled with babies. I could see heads and hands and tiny feet filling can after can. Some were still twitching and staring blankly. Some had burned skin. Others were not moving; their heads had been crushed. I could not move or speak when I saw them—I just stood there trembling in shock. I realized I was standing in an abortion clinic.

The Lord bent down to be close to His discarded friends. He turned to look up into my eyes and said, "Until your heart is torn like your flesh, you do not know how I feel about My friends. These are My friends."

I was standing there as another baby—a whole baby—was tossed by his leg into the trashcan. I could sense the Lord's thoughts as He saw this: "Silent and forgotten ones, you are not forgotten. You are *not* forgotten."

Although they were silent in that room, their screams echo throughout the corridors of eternity. Night and day they cry out, and their voices capture the ear of God Almighty.

I saw a man who had a torn heart, one who cried out for the babies. I knew that Heaven knows this man's name because he knows the Lord's friends. An unexpected proclamation burst from my heart toward this man: "You do not intercede in vain. Your name is known and your prayers are heard; it is not in vain."

Again the Lord looked into my eyes and said, "Until your heart is torn like your flesh is now, you do not know how I feel about My friends. You do not know Me."

It's Time to Dance

I felt wounded and exposed—wounded in my body and exposed in my heart. As I stood there sobbing, He got right in my face and said in a low whisper, "It's time to dance." With those perfect feet that tread the high places of the earth, He began dancing and stomping right in the middle of the abortion clinic. It was so powerful.

Each time when I was the most broken and the most undone, He would always say, "It's time to dance; it's time to war. To dance is to war." Then He would stomp with a new rhythm. It was not a feeble two-step or purposeless shuffling. The Judge was stomping out injustice with His very own feet. The dance was so full of intensity and authority that it seemed He took up all the air in the room.

He said, "Few have joined Me, but just wait until the earth joins Me in this dance. I am extending the invitation, but you can only dance when your heart is the most torn and broken."

Once again Jesus said, "I want you to meet some of My friends." We went straight through the earth yet again. I could barely stand after we emerged. My heart was broken and overwhelmed. My skin was torn. My body looked as if a bomb had exploded right next to me.

He led the way down a street, walking with determination. I wanted Him to walk slower because I was in so much pain, but my comfort was not His highest priority. He wanted me to feel the pain because He wanted my heart to know it, embrace it, and take it as my own so that I would better understand His heart.

He finally slowed His pace enough for me to walk beside Him. As we walked together, I realized that we were in Israel. At times, He tipped His head at people as if to say hello, but He never spoke. He would catch someone's eye and tip His head back to let the sun reveal His face. A small flame of understanding started to burn in the hearts of those at whom He looked, and their eyes would widen as they realized who He was. Jesus was opening the eyes of their hearts to see Him as the Messiah.

Some He tipped His head to were of great authority—the rabbis of the land and those with credibility within the Jewish community. I could see the Lord opening their eyes with nothing more than a glance. I knew He was appearing to some of the rabbis in the land, igniting the flame of revelation in their hearts.

...For what had not been told them they shall see, and what they had not heard they shall consider (Isaiah 52:15).

We invisibly followed these rabbis into private studies and quiet rooms of their homes. We watched them fall on their knees and cry out, "This changes everything, absolutely everything." The Lord knelt next to them and breathed on the tiny embers of revelation. Little by little, it started to burn and become like fire shut up in their bones.

Right now, they are hiding the fire of revelation and asking themselves if the encounters really did happen. But I saw that this fire would continue to burn until the appointed day when they can hold it in no longer. From the top of the mountains they will shout, "Yeshua is Messiah!"

Then I said, "I will not make mention of Him, nor speak anymore in His name." But His word was in my heart like a burning fire shut up in my bones; I was weary of holding it back, and I could not (Jeremiah 20:9).

I looked over and, for the first time, saw tears running down Jesus' face. I could hear Him sigh, "Oh, Jerusalem...Jerusalem."

Like Jacob loved Rachel and like Elkanah loved Hannah, I could feel the passion and love Jesus had for Israel. Yet His passion extended far beyond natural love, so He hurts more than a lover does when that love is not returned. He looked at me again and said, "Until your heart is torn like your skin is now, you do not know how I feel about My friends. You do not know Me."

I wept and the salt of my tears stung the wounds of my flesh, yet I could not stop crying. I crumpled to a heap on the floor, unable to stand under the weight of feeling His heart. He leaned down and whispered, "It is time to dance."

Suddenly we were in front of the Wailing Wall. He started dancing a tribal rhythm against injustice. I could feel the power of this dance. It was heavy and burning.

Jesus said, "A new dance will come out of worship and compassion for the poor of the earth. When your heart is the most broken for the forgotten—for those I call My friends—it is time to dance."

Chapter 20

Kneading Dough

God orchestrates our whole lives, with their many seasons, by con-
tinually pressing His Word into us. We experience great promotion
and great demotion, yet they both come from His hand. He invites to
us to stay steady and to embrace lovesickness for Jesus Christ regard-
less of the season in which we find ourselves (see Eccles. 3:1).

I had a dream. I saw the Lord take various ministries and
knead them individually as if they were bread dough. He turned
them inside out and pressed them over and over again. God had a
smile in His eyes, since He knew what the outcome of the kneading would be, even though the process might look unpleasant to an

outsider. He was maturing each ministry with its own identity and emphasis so it could be served to the nations.

I could see that various ministries were in the kneading process right now—everyone was being kneaded, from the core staff to those who are on the mere edges of the ministry—and that the season of baking in the fire was still to come. Particular ministries will be served to the nations like bread, but that will only happen after the Lord matures them through the seasons of kneading and baking.

Box Shaking

The scene and the appearance of the ministries changed. Now each ministry looked like a puzzle. I saw the Lord take hold of each ministry, one by one, and shake the puzzle box forcefully. "There is a shaking and a shift coming," He said. Then, with a smile on His face and delight in His eyes, He said five things as He continued shaking the boxes:

"I am moving those who have been in the front of the line to the back so they will learn the joy and delight of being at the end of the line.

"I am moving those who have been in the back of the line to the front so they learn to embrace humility and to work on excellence and skill. Those in the back of the line will be just as excellent and skillful as those in the front.

"But there are those at the front who already live by embracing the depths of humility; their positions will not be touched.

"There are those who, even at the back of the line, are filled with selfish ambition and pride; their positions at the back will not be touched.

"Those who feel they are irreplaceable will be the first ones replaced."

In the Lord's Kingdom, we get to the front by way of the back; we get to the top by way of the bottom. I saw some people who, even though they seemed to be following the Lord well, disqualified themselves from the calling or position the Lord had for them because of their lack of humility. And that was their choice. Because He loves them and is jealous for their hearts, God will not allow them to excel until they fully embrace the season they are in. Honor and respect are given only by God; they cannot be asked for or demanded. Only those who submit to the process of maturation and who are humble in all seasons will be exalted by God.

Humble yourselves in the sight of the Lord, and He will lift you up (James 4:10).

Chapter 21

The Sound of Abundant Rain

Have you ever considered that our Father in Heaven sees every tiny thing we do in secret? He knows every motive and intention we have. Whenever we make a secret choice to keep our life hidden in Him, it positions our hearts to receive more from the Lord and to give more of ourselves to the Lord.

*Then Elijah said to Ahab, "Go up, eat and drink; for there is **the sound of abundance of rain.**" So Ahab went up to eat and drink. And Elijah went up to the top of Carmel; then he bowed down on the ground, and put his face between his knees, and said to his servant,*

153

"Go up now, look toward the sea." So he went up and looked, and said, "There is nothing." And seven times he said, "Go again." Then it came to pass the seventh time, that he said, "There is a cloud, as small as a man's hand, rising out of the sea!" So he said, "Go up, say to Ahab, 'Prepare your chariot, and go down before the rain stops you'" (1 Kings 18:41-44).

I had a dream. I was in the middle of the ocean running on waves. In the distance, I could see that a small cloud in the sky was set in motion—it was coming toward me. I'd never seen a cloud that looked like this one. It was the most shiny, sparkling blue I had ever seen. I began yelling over and over, "There's a cloud in the sky the size of a man's hand! There's a cloud in the sky the size of a man's hand!"

A worship team was near me, bobbing up and down like a ship at sea. I understood this to mean that the cloud arose out of worship.

Two Scriptures were highlighted to me at this point.

...Even the night shall be light about me (Psalm 139:11).

But you, when you pray, go into your room, and when you have shut your door, pray to your Father who is in the secret place; and your Father who sees in secret will reward you openly (Matthew 6:6).

The Lord showed me what would happen when the rain fell. I saw the pursuits to which people were giving themselves in secret, whether good or bad. I knew they would publicly give themselves to these efforts with their full energy when the rain came. The coming rain was a catalyst to propel each person along whatever path he or she was already on. Some would receive the rain as grace. Others were offended by it and further hardened their hearts, leading to judgment—yet both situations were invitations from the Lord to give our lives to Him.

Some had already chosen to give themselves to true life. Their secret lives were hidden in Christ. Everything they did was done in secret unto God. Even when the rains came, these people were all the more focused on staying faithful to the Lord under His gaze. They were unmoved by promotion. Many want to be seen as faithful in their visible affairs without aligning their private lives toward faithfulness at the same time; but it is important to God that we are utterly faithful in the small things when no one is watching.

I could see God's eyes watching us and everything we did— yes, everything. He was overcome with joy when He saw our faithfulness in the small things, in the mundaneness of life.

Some had already chosen to give their lives to death. When the rain came, the things they were doing in secret affected who they became in a greater way. The rain did not suddenly change who they were or make them holy; it only encouraged them to publicly become who they already were inside. Their secret lives were shown before God and before man.

You have set our iniquities before You, our secret sins in the light of Your countenance (Psalm 90:8).

Then in my dream I started yelling, "Grace like rain is falling. Come, grace! Grace like rain is falling." I understood this to mean that rains come in the Spirit to all of us. Those who give themselves to true life will thrive; those who give themselves to anything less will receive their selfish ambitions. God is giving time and grace for us to recommit, ask Him for mercy, and confess our sins to one another so we can be free.

The cloud in the sky may not look any bigger than a man's hand, but there is a season of intense rain coming. Because God has such passion for us to rid ourselves of sin, He is inviting us to greater faithfulness in secret.

Chapter 22

When Justice Rolls, Go Low

In this dream, I saw the throne room of Heaven as described in Revelation 4. Through this dream I could see the importance of "going low" before the majesty of God and the necessity of wearing humility as a garment day by day, minute by minute, second by second. The God of eternal burning is pleased to answer the cry of His people who, in all humility and confidence, have set their hearts to cry out to Him. Let us set our hearts all the more to "go low in all humility." As justice flows like a river from the throne of God, let us go low so as not to be consumed.

I had a dream. I was standing in Heaven on the glassy sea before God's throne. I could see the throne some distance away. It was above the sea and there was One sitting on it.

All of Heaven was so rhythmic. I could hear the waves of the crystal sea crashing. The sound was so loud and bright that it hurt my ears. The tide that came in made a sound all its own, different from the tide that went out. It was the sound of water and the sound of glass at the same time—as if the water was a glassy tide flowing in and out from around the throne.

I could see a green rainbow around the throne—the mercy of God. The color itself was thick, as if it had substance and energy within it. I had never seen that color of green before. His mercy gave my soul such boldness to approach the throne, and yet I also felt the fear of the Lord as I watched wave after wave of mercy pulse outward from this One seated on the throne.

I think I was standing on the sea because I don't remember seeing its edge, but I did know that the tide was flowing in and out underneath me. Everything was moving, never stopping, always in constant motion—up and down, back and forth, round and round—as the tide of the crystal sea flowed in and out.

And deep within me I kept hearing, "Justice rolls like a river. Justice rolls like a river."

> *But let justice roll on like a river, righteousness like a never-failing stream!* (Amos 5:24 NIV)

I looked up and saw a stream of living water intertwined with a river of fire flowing from the center of the throne. The water that flowed was wrapped in fire, and the fire itself was flowing. All at once, I realized I was looking at a scene from the Book of Daniel:

> *A fiery stream issued and came forth from before Him. A thousand thousands ministered to Him; ten thousand times ten thousand*

stood before Him. The court was seated, and the books were opened (Daniel 7:10).

Over the sound of the rushing water and fire, I could hear the sound of wings. At a distance, I could see extraordinary creatures—seraphim—with eyes all over their bodies. Each eye was opened wide with awe; the One on the throne transfixed them. They stared at Him continually as if it was the first time they had seen anything so magnificent and beautiful. The creatures kept circling the throne and the sound of their wings made a steady rhythm...up and down and up and down, smooth and constant, roaring and fearful, never ceasing. I realized the creatures had been doing this since the beginning of time, yet they still could not get enough of gazing at the One on His throne.

I could hear the sound of crowns rolling on the floor of Heaven as the 24 elders cast down their many crowns. They do not lay them down or set them down gently. They cast their crowns in awesome, adoring agony, as if to throw every bit of their being, worth, and energy before this One who is so holy. They cast their crowns gladly, for He is worthy of their worship.

I heard a voice that came from the throne. I do not know if it was God or an angel, but it was the loudest sound I have ever heard. I felt like I was right underneath a 100-foot glass wave that was going to crash down on me at any moment.

Nowhere to Hide

I felt like I could not go low enough. I wanted the sea to swallow me up. I was quite a distance away from the throne, but I felt like I was right up close. I tried to dive under the waves or swim far enough away from the throne so I could not be found—anywhere but there—but I was unable to move. There was nowhere to go or hide, though I kept trying.

And still, I was aware of Heaven's constant movement: the living creatures rhythmically beating their wings...the sound of living waters intertwined with the sound of burning fire...the ebb and flow of the crashing sea...the rumbling vibration of the crowns...

All the while, I kept hearing, "Justice rolls like a river. Justice rolls like a river."

I could see a huge book with a huge hand touching its cover, preparing to open it. It was the hand that spanned the stars and marked off the heavens, the One who measures the waters in the hollow of His hand (see Isa. 23:11; 40:12). I could not read the title of the book. A message was spoken and a huge angel flew from the throne toward me. I thought this angel was going to knock me over, but instead he flew right through me.

I looked down and I could see planet Earth. Many heavenly beings were watching humankind constantly; there was much activity happening between Heaven and earth. Like shooting stars that streak across the sky, angels were descending toward the earth. I knew these heavenly messengers were being loosed to earth in a significant way. Something was almost ready to happen—new spiritual seasons were coming to the Body of Christ—although I did not know the details.

ON OUR KNEES

Then I saw the Lord pick up a huge wick and drop it to earth. The wick had three strands entwined together. He stuck the other end of the wick in the river of fire and living water that flowed out from His throne. The wick began to burn, starting in Heaven and moving slowly toward earth.

As the people on earth watched the flame coming slowly toward them, some went low and prostrated themselves before God in humble worship. Others saw the approaching flame but did not go low. Those who remained standing were burned like coal; they were consumed by this fire.

I kept asking, "Why?" And I kept hearing, "Go low. Go low in all humility. Pray. As justice rolls, go low. As justice rolls, go low."

When justice rolls from the throne, the only safe place to be is on our knees with hearts that are not offended. When we are offended, we stand up and stiffen our backs, but lovers bow low.

I was so enveloped by what I was seeing that I had to be shaken out of it. The Lord gave me understanding of why I was seeing these scenes of heavenly activity, bringing to my mind two verses about humility. It was so clear, like the finger of God was writing it on my heart.

> *Then he said to me, "Do not fear, Daniel, for from the first day that you set your heart to understand, and to humble yourself before your God, your words were heard; and I have come because of your words"* (Daniel 10:12).

> *The humble He guides in justice, and the humble He teaches His way* (Psalm 25:9).

Then the Lord spoke to my heart, saying, "Press in all the more in humility, for My justice is surely beginning. The fire straight from My throne has been lit."

And as I looked at the seraphim and elders surrendering themselves in worship again and again, I kept hearing, "When justice rolls, go low. Go low so as not to be consumed."

The Lord gives grace to the needy, mercy to the humble, opportunity to those who resist, and an invitation to all. He is slow to anger and rich in love. If we bow low in humility, He will meet us there.

Chapter 23

A Card Game

The Lord is always asking us to trust Him and to give Him total control. To be honest, I sometimes feel I can do it better—my plans seem so perfect. But then I feel the prodding of the Holy Spirit to turn it over to Him. He is always stirring my faith in new ways, but the act of turning things over is just so difficult. That's why this dream means a lot to me: His promise to us is that He has set us up to win. This can be an invitation to lay down the smallest things or the greatest things. The spiritual man in this dream is "all" of us for we all need to learn this lesson. In this life, we win by laying it all down.

Lord, help me today to turn over all control. Help me trust You.

I had a dream. I was invited to watch a card game. Jesus was sitting at a card table shuffling a deck of cards. He invited a spiritual man to play, but I could tell by the man's expression that he was not very comfortable with the game. He was unsure how it would turn out. Jesus had a twinkle in His eyes and a smile on His face. I mean He literally had a beam of white light in the center of the black pupil of His eye. Jesus was already seated at the table, ready to play the game, not even looking to see if the man was going to join Him; He knew he would.

I shouldn't have been, but I was surprised at how well Jesus began to shuffle the deck of cards. The things He did would have made any card shark look like a novice. Without looking up, He began to deal the cards. The Lord said to the man, "Sit down and relax. Let's play a game of cards. Winner takes all."

He said, "Listen closely. I have stacked the deck in your favor. I have set it up for you to win the hand." With a small chuckle at His own joke, He said, "But I promise it is not fifty-two card pick-up." Then His eyes twinkled even more as He continued, "It is the hand that leads straight to Acts 4."

THE DECK IS STACKED

The man sat down, still looking a bit uncomfortable, as the Lord dealt out five cards. The man quickly realized the deck really was stacked in his favor: he held an ace, king, queen, jack, and ten. On each card were also written the fivefold ministry gifts from Ephesians 4:11. He thought to himself, *I have a straight.*

Again the Lord said, "Now, here are the rules. I have stacked the deck in your favor, but in order for you to win, you must hand over to Me all of your aces, kings, queens, jacks, and tens."

The man looked at his cards, thinking, "Well, I could just turn over the ten and keep the rest." The Lord, knowing the man's thoughts, looked into his eyes and said, "It doesn't work like that. I do not want just one card, I want your whole hand. You will receive the full house if you turn over the whole hand."

So, one by one, very slowly, the man turned over each of the cards. As he placed them in the center of the table, to his amazement, written across each card was the word *control* in large, bold, red letters.

The Lord stretched out His hand and began to pick up the cards the man had laid down. He said, "You only have a winning hand when I hold all the cards. I want total control of the deck. I want control over the highs and the lows, the good and the bad. This is how you get a winning hand, this is how you win the game, and this is the way Acts 4 will become a modern reality—when I hold all of the cards."

Chapter 24

A Change of Color

During worship at a large church conference in Atlanta, Georgia, I felt like I stepped into a vision. It was so clear to me that I instinctively started singing what I was seeing. After I was faithful to sing out the vision, I began to understand the meaning of what I was viewing.

I had a vision. I saw the blood of black slaves calling from the ground. The sound swelled more and more until I realized that it was more than words—it was singing. I heard black spirituals with rhythm and words that tumbled over each other for a few moments. It seemed as if each song was jostling with the others to be heard, pushing and pulling the syncopation in all directions.

But finally, all the spirituals came together with the same pulse. I understood that at the time these spirituals were originally sung, they were the "new song" that literally kept the slaves steady. The words and rhythms gave them strength within, helped them keep their pace, and filled them with hope.

The unified cadence pushed me, and I began singing, "God has not forgotten the cries and the songs of the slaves who lifted their voices to God, even in death."

AN ALL-CONSUMING FIRE

As the black spirituals pulsed, I saw fires in Atlanta that were lit during the Civil War. Then I saw many new fires coming to Atlanta and to the South, but this was not a repeat of the Civil War. It was an all-consuming fire coming with healing and to break down the walls that separate one person and one race from another.

Starting in the South and spreading like an uncontrolled wildfire throughout the nation, a small flicker of the all-consuming fire began to touch African American men and women. When they were touched, they sang out a song of righteousness and praise to God. The more they sang, the more the fire grew within them and the more light was released. And as they shone with righteousness, they began to take their places of leadership in the Body of Christ.

I kept singing, "This time when the fire comes, the walls will surely fall down between races, and there will be a change of color in the leadership at the helm." I understood that the African American community will lead the way in a righteous worship movement that will bring revival to the nations.

Chapter 25

His Instrument

The Lord is coming to release the most beautiful of sounds. He is going to be singing beautiful, fresh, new songs through His Bride and the prayer movement in the earth. The Chief Musician has saved the best songs for these days, and in this season He is coming to tune His instruments—you and me—so we will sing the New Song so many will see Him, fear Him, and put their trust in Him alone (see Ps. 40).

I had a dream. In my dream I was asleep but was startled awake by a terrible sound. It was the sound of someone strumming a guitar, but each string was horribly out of tune. The grating sound made me want to place my hands over my ears and yell, "Stop!"

I sat up in my bed and saw an angel seated at the foot of the bed with a guitar. I could not get close enough to see his face, but I noticed the guitar was dusty and old and had some scratches on it. It had apparently been used often but was not taken care of as it should have been. The angel was strumming the old guitar, but the strings were loose and not in tune. I was perplexed why the angel kept trying to play this old, useless guitar.

The angel did not look at me but kept his eyes on the guitar. Even through the irritating sound, I could tell he was happy just holding it. I thought to myself, *You are an angel. Why are you playing that? You could play anything, any instrument imaginable, but you are trying to play an old guitar—and it sounds terrible. You must not be a musical angel.* Yet, still he strummed. This went on for several minutes. He was not at all concerned with how bad the sound was, and he had no intention of leaving my bedroom.

Tightening the Strings

Then, ever so slowly, as if waiting for the precise moment in time, the angel began tightening the strings on the guitar. In fact, he began to draw each string so tight that I watched the process through squinted eyes, prepared for the neck of the old guitar to snap in two at any moment. With the slow, deliberate movements of each finger, the angel took further control of the instrument.

I tried offering advice, telling him a better way to prepare the strings. "Excuse me, but you're going to break your guitar. You might not want to strain the strings and the neck like that." But he paid me no attention; he was not going to tune any other way than his own.

When each string was seated correctly and pulled tight, he began the process of tuning each one. I was amazed because I thought the strings could not stretch any further; he proved they could.

I could tell this instrument moved him. He handled it with gentleness and purpose, like it was an old friend with a new lease on life. He tuned the strings by playing the harmonics of each string. Even while tuning, he made sounds come from his instrument that I did not know were possible.

When the last string sang out its perfect tone, he took his hands from the guitar and clasped them together as if resting them from the strain of tightening the strings. He flexed his wrists and then, gently, placed each finger on the taut strings—and he played.

A New Song

He played a new song, a new melody. He knew exactly where He was going with each strum.

I was shocked. It was the most beautiful sound I have ever experienced. The music moved through me. It had substance and carried meaning and emotion. There is nothing I know of to compare it to—no sound or sense matches what I felt when I heard him play.

As he played the old guitar, it was as if I was hearing a Stradivarius. Song after song, every rhythm and measure was flawless. The strings—once pulled tightly and perfectly tuned—made the most beautiful sound, and I did not want it to end. I just wanted to experience this beautiful sound all night.

In a moment I went from thinking, *What a terrible sound,* to the extreme opposite. It was beyond words.

This is when I noticed his skill was that of a master musician, so I leaned in to get a good look at him. Just then, it was as if a column of starlight came through my window and I was able to see his face.

THE MASTER MUSICIAN

He was no angel at all. It was Jesus, the Chief Musician. It suddenly seemed—like two dancers in perfect rhythm or like the heat from light—that the guitar was merely an extension of Him.

He refused to be distracted from His work. He knew the guitar would not break. He knew what He was doing: playing a new sound that had been in His heart for some time. He knew the sound his guitar was capable of producing, and He would not stop until it made the sound for which it was created.

Listening to the melodies, I knew in an instant that He is coming to *tune* His Bride. He is coming to stretch His Bride and the prayer movement in the earth. He is coming to tighten the strings of our hearts. And just when it feels like our strings can't be tightened any more lest they snap—well, then He is going to tighten them some more.

He will bend us and stretch us until He sees that each string is in perfect harmony with His heart. Then the Master Himself is going to play us. He is going to release the *new* through us. It will be the most beautiful sound in the earth. He will tune us, and we will be His Stradivarius. We will be His instrument. All we do is let the Master Musician have His way in our lives, and He will play His song through us to the nations of the earth.

And it truly is a sound as revealed in Psalm 40:3 that has a fresh, new meaning, *"He has put a new song in my mouth—praise to our God; many will see it and fear, and will trust in the LORD."*

Chapter 26

A City Within a City

In this dream, I believe I saw what some cities of refuge will look like. I loved being able to see them. I could see that these cities of refuge will function as cities within a city.

I had a dream. I saw cities of refuge—each of which became labeled "A City Within a City"—begin to arise in the earth. It was as if each of these communities was its own city within its own city, complete with stores, food, and social structure. It seemed the world was dark, but these "cities of refuge" were not looking to the world for answers. They were not overtaken by the surrounding spiritual darkness. They were divinely protected by God's favor from what was happening in the world. What was happening in the world was dark and there was not enough food or medical care. This was not the case in the arising cities of refuge.

These cities of refuge were not cities unto themselves, for they began to take on the type of fasting mentioned in Isaiah 58. They reached out to the poor. Even when large worldly cities in themselves could not take care of their own, somehow the cities within the city—the cities of refuge—always had enough like in First Kings 4.

ALWAYS ENOUGH

These cities had arms that reached out to the poor, the out-casts, the sick, and the lost. When large cities in the natural couldn't handle the need, when they could not take care of their own, the cities of refuge were able to take care of all. There were medical facilities open to the community. When the local government could not help and did not have economic and medical resources or plans, they sent people to "the city within the city." When hopeless medical words were pronounced, then even the lost and those out of covenant with God made their way to the cities of refuge.

I saw that God will greatly bless in this manner; I saw there were many cities worldwide on which God will pour out the same favor.

I saw a change concerning creative and journalistic media that will come from these cities of refuge. All types of media were released in waves that were more expansive than anything I had ever seen. In fact, the means of releasing information to the public increased at a dramatic rate as well. The media created in these cities was broadcast globally and covered everything from movies and concerts to news and television shows—every category of media.

I also saw a house of prayer right in the middle of each city. A white smoke was rising that was visible to the whole of each city and beyond. The smoke was as white as could be and ascended as continual incense. It never stopped; it was always ascending. It was as if every person who lived outside of the walls of the city of refuge was reminded by the continual white smoke arising that there was prayer arising to God on behalf of the city.

Chapter 27

The Fear of the Lord

Do you know how God controls the clouds and makes His lightning flash? Do you know how the clouds hang poised, those wonders of Him who is perfect in knowledge? ...Out of the north He comes in golden splendor; God comes in awesome majesty. The Almighty is beyond our reach and exalted in power; in His justice and great righteousness, He does not oppress. Therefore, men revere Him, for does He not have regard for all the wise in heart? (Job 37:15-16;22-24 NIV)

I had a dream. I had just parked my car at the International House of Prayer parking lot and I was headed inside. As I stepped out of the car, to my amazement, I saw a large angel standing on top of the building roof. He looked to be about 30 feet tall. This angel stood on the corner of the building with a sword in His hand, pointing directly to the north. He did not move but only pointed, resolute as a statue. The sword was shimmering. It was brilliant and shining.

I turned in the direction that He was pointing His sword. As I looked to the north, I saw the sun rising—from the north rather than the usual east. It was bizarre and beautiful. I had never seen anything like this before in my life. The sun was huge—at least seven times as big as it should have been. It was yellow, red, and orange—the brightest of hot colors—and it seemed to expand across the sky without restraint.

The gigantic sun and the breathtaking colors across the sky reminded me of Psalm 19:4-5:

> ...In them He has set a tabernacle for the sun, which is like a bridegroom coming out of his chamber, and rejoices like a strong man to run its race.

I felt the heat of the sun on my face.

I found myself looking back and forth between the angel pointing at the sky in the north and then looking at this giant sun full of the most vibrant colors. As I turned again and began to study the angel holding his glimmering sword, I saw carved across the sword five words in bold, black letters: **The Fear of the Lord.** The angel held his sword so assertively. He did not shy away from those words. He was bolstered by what they meant—the angel knew who God was.

In an instant, I knew that the Fear of the Lord was coming *into* His house. The awe of God was arising in a new way throughout the earth and in His Body.

At that moment I was reminded of Exodus 20:20: *"...that His fear may be before you, so that you may not sin."* Deep within my heart I heard the Holy Spirit say, "The fear of the Lord is coming. The awe of the God of Israel is arising in the midst of the prayer movement. It is arising in the midst of My House."

All this happened even before I was inside the building. So when I walked through the front door of the prayer room, I was surprised to come face to face with a mountain that was veiled by dense fog.

The Great Mountain

Not every person was allowed to walk up this great mountain. Only those with clean hands and pure hearts. Everyone not allowed to ascend stood and looked up at the great, hidden mountain, wondering what was beyond the haze.

With great anticipation I began my journey. In silence, I and others ascended high into the cloud of gray, heavy vapor, unsure of what we would find or where we would stop. We could see only the next single step in front of us. In the cool breeze, I soon lost the sense that anyone else was with me.

As I approached the top of the mountain, I realized I was literally walking up the mountain of the Lord. I was *in* Psalm 24. I was ascending up and up and up.

I had to set my heart for the journey. It was not easy but I could not stop walking up and up and up. I was walking on a narrow path, which reminded me of Matthew 7:14, and I thought, *Strive to stay on the narrow path.* It was a path well-trodden and I pondered the patriarchs of old who had walked the same path.

I was carrying some baggage with me, but I realized I would never make it to the top of the mountain if I kept it with me, so I took it off and laid it down. Many people around me didn't want to remove their baggage. Because they wanted to keep it, they were unable to ascend. They stopped and started walking back down the mountain.

Only One Path

I came upon an elderly man with a rod in his right hand. He had a long, white beard and long, wild, white hair that fell down over his shoulders. I noticed his face was set to go up. He was not looking to the left or the right; His face was set. He was not turning around or even grumbling about the steepness of the path. I saw people in front of him begin to look for shortcuts or different paths. They walked off the path trying to find an easier way up the mountain.

The elderly man said, "There are no shortcuts and there are no other paths. There is only one way, and it is this path. If you stay on it, it will lead you straight to the top." As he spoke, his words penetrated the very core of my heart, and I kept telling myself, *Stay on the path, there are no shortcuts, keep walking, keep walking.*

Then I happened to see a road sign: The Pathway of Humility. At that exact moment I realized I was actually walking this path with Moses—the elderly man was Moses. In an instant my eyes were open to see the humility, the diligence, and the zeal of this man who had great authority and presence. He continued up the mountain saying over and over, "There are no short cuts and there are no other paths. There is only one way and it is this path. If you stay on it, it will lead you straight to the top."

No Shortcuts

Finally, as we ascended to the very top of the magnificent mountain, I saw men and women standing at the very top and crying out Psalm 24:7, *"Lift up your heads, O you gates! And be lifted up, you everlasting doors! And the King of glory shall come in."* I realized that I was standing in a place of great authority. This is the place where we have the authority to cry out, *"Lift up your heads, O you gates!"*

Many people get this invitation, but few make the whole journey. Many of us start this journey with baggage, and during this great trek up the mountain of the Lord, we lay our baggage aside and continue to walk upward. But many people want to keep their baggage and they are unable to continue their journeys. Some people wandered off the trodden path for other adventures.

I knew this was not a sight-seeing tour. This was the real thing—I was ascending the mountain of the Lord to receive a new authority that the Fear of the Lord would be released.

I saw that there were no shortcuts to the top of this mountain. It is easier to just stay on the path and keep walking. This is the invitation of the Lord to climb His Holy Mountain with clean hands and a pure heart. Though some people start with baggage, we all have the opportunity to lay it down.

The pathway called Humility is the way to the top, and the top is where we are granted the authority to proclaim Psalm 24:7, *"Lift up your heads, O you gates! And be lifted up, you everlasting doors! And the King of glory shall come in."*

When I awoke from this dream. I felt as if I had walked on a journey all night long, but I felt energized and refreshed with a new zeal for righteousness and the ability to set my heart on humility. I felt a new season where the Holy Spirit is coming to us with the gift of the Fear of the Lord.

His fear, His awe, is coming into our lives, our church services, our prayer meetings like a mist—a weighty presence. Some places will actually have a tangible mist evidenced in their meetings. I believe this is a heads-up that the awe of God, the Fear of the Lord is close at hand. It is His gift and His invitation for us to ascend

His spiritual mountain with clean hands and pure hearts—with righteous actions and holy desires.

He is coming into our midst again with glorious splendor and the Fear of the Lord. The hosts of Heaven know His glory and awesome majesty, and they are announcing it to the earth—and they will announce it to the earth through us, His Bride.

Chapter 28

The Book of Me

You number my wanderings; put my tears into Your bottle; are they not in Your book? When I cry out to You, then my enemies will turn back; this I know, because God is for me (Psalm 56:8-9).

I had a dream. I was back in school and sitting in the second row of a classroom. There was no one else in the class. I was very excited because when I looked up to the front of class, I saw my favorite teacher was teaching—Jesus. I was really excited because no one else was in this class, so I had Him all to myself.

Jesus came to the front row of seats and turned a chair around toward me so He was sitting right in front of me. With a sparkle in

His eyes and a smile big on His face, He laid a book on my desk. It was a large, tan book with a title in bold, black letters: **The Book of Me.**

I opened this book ever so carefully and with great suspense. To my amazement, I found written in words the story of my life. This really was *The Book of Me*. It was my life. I noticed the pages of this book were a pale yellow. It was thick old paper with ridges on the edges of each page. Each word has been detailed and written by a quill and ink. I remember thinking that someone went to great length to record my comings and goings in life; and as I read, it seemed like everything was written in the pages of this book.

It was not an account of my *sins*, it was a record of my *choices*. As I began to read through some of the chapters, I thought of King David when he said:

> *You number my wanderings; put my tears into Your bottle; are they not in Your book?* (Psalm 56:8)

As I flipped through this book about me, each word on the page began to sink into my soul. Suddenly an overwhelming sensation of pure love engulfed me, and I realized He saw everything. He saw every choice I made in secret and it was written down. He took notice of the tiny choices to the great choices. Everything was written down and every choice remembered. Here they were—altogether in *The Book of Me*—nothing had escaped His watchful gaze.

Every Choice Recorded

I saw a graph of my life and the choices I had made. As I looked at the seasons of my life, I could almost go back to that season and see how I set my heart, what God had done inside of me, and how my choices had pleased the Father or how my choices had prepared the way for me to go through the same season again.

God was never worried about bad choices because He would set things up again and again so that I would make the right choices. If I made a wrong choice, well, then God would allow me go through the season again and again. He didn't get mad or frustrated at my choices, but with a big smile He would set up the season for me to go through again so that I could make the right choice. I could see that God gave (and still gives) me the opportunity to make the right choices for Him.

As I continued to read through the book of my life, I noticed that even childhood choices that I had totally forgotten were recorded—like the time when I was 5 years of age and I wanted God to know that I loved Him. I wrote Him a note and then I went into my front yard and held it up high. I was expecting dozens of angels to come through the clouds, grab my note, and take it back to God in Heaven. Well, nothing happened and the note stayed in my hands. I went back inside my house and cried because I thought, *How will God know that I love Him? He didn't read my note.*

I had forgotten about that incident until I read it in *The Book of Me.* But, God had numbered it, and that small thing I did as a child was written in the book. Every thought was written down. Now that was hard to read. I didn't realize the extent of my thoughts and how God hears everything. It was as if I could see a picture of Psalm 139:4, *"For there is not a word on my tongue, but behold, O LORD, You know it altogether."* Well, that means good and bad. In Psalm 19:14 (NIV) David says, *"May the words of my mouth and the meditation of my heart be pleasing in Your sight, O LORD, my Rock and my Redeemer."*

Every single memory, trial, thought, choice, good day, bad day, hard day, fun day, frustrating day, sad day—there they were before me noticed and written on the pages of this book. The words were actually life to my soul as I was reading, and I felt myself getting stronger and stronger by the story of my very own life. It was not a condemning history of my life but one of conviction and encouragement from the good choices. This made me want to read on and on. Oh, how our right and wise choices make the Father's heart glad even when they seem so small!

Heart Responses

I noticed that *bad* things were not written in this book. Even when I had made a wrong choice, I saw that it was an opportunity for the season to come again so I could make the right choice for God the next time. He is always about restoration.

As I looked at each page, skillfully written and accurately telling the journey of my heart responses, I was so encouraged for my next season. I was thinking, *I can really do this...I can do this!*

I kept turning the pages of the book and I noticed that the last half of the book had blank pages. I wondered, *Where's the rest?* I know that the Lord knows our future. He knows everything. He was inviting me to set my heart to steady in a whole new way.

The Lord looked right into my eyes and said:
"Remember this:

1. Every season is a gateway to the next—end each season well.

2. Every season of new favor and authority should always lead to a heart response of great humility and servanthood."

And then, leaning into me even closer and looking into my eyes, He said, "Always remember, I am as close as the air you breathe. You are never out of the gaze of My eyes."

Then suddenly He vanished, and I was sitting there in my dream still holding *The Book of Me*, touching the roughness of the pages, reading about my journey and my heart, and saying to my own heart, *Julie, end each season well. Each season in life is a gateway to the next. You can do this.*

Then as quickly as the dream started, it was over. I woke up saying to myself, *End well...end each season well. Make this season a good season. This will one day be my history, so make it a good history.*

PSALM 56

After this dream, I kept pondering over and over Psalm 56. I love that Scripture passage. As I began to study it, I found this interesting excerpt in C. H. Spurgeon's *The Treasury of David*:

> Every step which the fugitive (David) had taken (when pursued by his enemies), was not only observed but thought worthy of counting and recording. We perhaps are so confused after a long course of trouble, that we hardly know where we have or where we have not been; but our considerate Father remembers all in detail; for he has counted them over as men count their gold, for even the trial of our faith is precious in his sight.[1]

David actually wrote Psalm 56 when the Philistines had captured him at Gath. The enemy had captured David, yet he began to write, "Even here, God, You number my wanderings. You tell of my paths. Even here You have kept all of my tears in your bottle, and even here everything is written in Your book" (see Ps. 56:8). David somehow saw into the spiritual dimension of what was happening. He knew that God was with him and not mad at him and was actually "for" him, as we see in verse 9 where David says, "... *This I know, because God is for me.*"

ENDNOTE

1. C. H. Spurgeon, *The Treasury of David* (Grand Rapids, MI: Kregel Publications, 2004).

Chapter 29

God's Arising Media Army

*In the beginning God created the heavens and the earth. The earth was without form, and void; and darkness was on the face of the deep. And the Spirit of God was **hovering** over the face of the waters* (Genesis 1:1-2).

I love these verses in Genesis 1. One of the words that stands out to me is *hovering*. I picture the Spirit of God *bursting forth with passion to create*, almost as if the Spirit of God is pulsing like a heartbeat and ready to create. Suddenly something new was bursting forth. I have been gripped by this Scripture because today I see the Spirit of God doing the same thing. He is hovering; He is bursting with excitement to yet again create, to birth the new on the earth.

Matthew Henry's Commentary on this particular verse says the following, "God is not only the author of all being, but the fountain of life and the *spring of motion*."

God is the "spring of motion" for the new that He is releasing to the earth, and God's heart is to topple the mountain of media as we know it today. He is stirring His Bride and the prayer movement in the earth in happy holiness and joyful righteousness. We need to be a people wholly given to the Lord and to His purposes, those who embrace the lowest place so God will have His way in us and through us. He will use yielded vessels in magnificent ways in the coming days.

David speaks several times in the Book of Psalms to "sing to the Lord a new song."

> *Rejoice in the LORD, O you righteous! For praise from the upright is beautiful. Praise the LORD with the harp; make melody to Him with an instrument of ten strings.* **Sing to Him a new song;** *play skillfully with a shout of joy* (Psalm 33:1-3).

That word *new* means *fresh, new thing.* I feel this invitation from the Lord for the new, the fresh is coming, and God is going to sing His song, write His script, paint His picture, and dance His dance through a Bride who is lovesick. A Bride who is not in it for money or personal fame—but for the fame of His glorious name. A Bride who is steadfast in the place of prayer.

WORLDWIDE MEDIA

I know this because I had a dream. I was sitting with the Ancient of Days, and He had opened before Him the checkbook of finance. He was writing a check, and He was singing a song:

This is why I'm gonna write the check.
This is why I'm gonna give you the money.
It's the Great Invitation to the divine interruption in
media. . .media. . .media.

The word *media* resounded from every direction like an echo.

I saw a worldwide media force spring up, and the prayer room will fuel it. God is going to have His way in every facet of media as long as people are driven by prayer and passion for Him and their "one thing" continues to be passion for God and prayer. I noticed that there was no ceiling as to where or how high this media will go.

I felt like God somehow transported me to the future. In the dream, I was sitting in a movie theater and all around me people were crying. The Lord was pouring out the Spirit of Wisdom and Revelation and people were getting saved *at the movies.*

THE NEW MEDIA

In the dream, I was in a bar, and when the new song began to play, people who were drinking away their sorrows put down their drinks. They began to weep because of the anointing upon the music. As the music played, the anointing that was on David when he played his harp before Saul and drove out the evil spirits—this same ancient anointing—filled the bar, and salvation was poured out in the middle of the new song in the bar.

I was there. I could see it and feel it. When the new song was being played, there was a heavy weight of the presence of God even in the bar, and people were giving their lives to the Lord right there. *This is the effect that the new music will have.*

A shift and a flip is going to happen in the media and it will be God's doing. God is going to give the awards of the world to the righteous. There will be number 1 hit songs that come out of houses of prayer and God's media centers. God is going to raise up something totally new. God wants to touch the ends of the earth through media and music.

I saw a shift happen. What worked yesterday will no longer work today. The shift will scramble today's media because what is arising is something that cannot be copied or bought with a price because it is the *anointing behind* the media and the sound that is making it happen.

When lovesick worshipers are not moved by anything except passion for Jesus and intercession, this passion will lead their hearts straight into what is *new* in music, television, computer games, video games, all types of recordings, Broadway, art, dance, and every facet of media.

GOD'S MEDIA CENTERS

I saw huge downloads exploding in the minds of those who wait on the Lord (see Isa. 40:31). I saw painters being given new colors to paint with. I saw colors in Heaven that the earth has not yet seen. They were florescent and the paint contained a shine and a glow that will greatly surpass anything that the world has seen.

I saw the Lord give strategies for computer games and video games. I was watching young boys and girls play computer games that were leading them into the knowledge of God. In the midst of the games, I could see *Revelation* awaken in their young minds and hearts.

I saw in the dream that the day is coming when people will no longer turn to the news of the world—they will tune in to God's media centers to see what God is saying because of the clarity of the Word of God released through the prayer movement in the earth. The news media as we know it today will more and more sell out to what people want, and they will become full of lies and celebrity gossip. However, I did see a major television network hop on board to join God's media army.

There is a divine switch coming in:

- Print and Broadcast Media
- Movies/Film
- Music
- Art
- Dance
- Games
- Theater/Broadway

God is doing something new and in new geographical places. I saw different hubs all over the United States. I saw them in Kansas City, Nashville, Phoenix, Palm Springs, and Charlotte, North Carolina. There will be media centers in many places; these were the ones I saw in the dream.

After I had this dream, I was invited by my friend Joshua Mills to be part of "Heaven Invading Hollywood"—a night of worship right at the gates of Paramount Pictures. As I walked around the back lot of Paramount Pictures, I felt as if I was walking in my dream, as I had already been there. I was walking around the back lots and studios that I had dreamed. I was in amazement and I knew God was up to something.

It's the great invitation to the divine interruption in media, and you are invited to be part of the greatest show on earth.

Chapter 30

The Big, Blue, Beautiful, Rushing, Gushing River

Then he said to me: "This water flows toward the eastern region, goes down into the valley, and enters the sea. When it reaches the sea, its waters are healed. And it shall be that every living thing that moves, wherever the rivers go, will live. There will be a very great multitude of fish, because these waters go there; for they will be healed, and everything will live wherever the river goes (Ezekiel 47:8-9).

I had a dream. I was standing right beside the beautiful river mentioned in Ezekiel 47. The river was rushing, it was gushing, and it was like clear, blue crystal. I could see *way* in the distance that it was flowing from an opening, like a portal, in the sky as if it was flowing down from the very throne of God. There were orbs of light that followed this river from the sky to the earth and all through its flowing.

I found myself thinking, *Could this be the river that Ezekiel himself saw?* I was looking at these mighty waters rush by me like a torrent of flowing water. It was as if these waters were alive and they flowed with a purpose to touch and heal everything; for everywhere these waters go shall be healing for body, soul, mind, and spirit.

I wish I could describe the beauty of this color blue—blue that also looked like sapphire crystals. The river looked like a sparkling jewel, yet the river was water, like oil dripping down my hand. There was no stopping it, but at the same time, people could get in the river and not drown.

I saw Bob Jones, a prophetic father to many spiritual movements in the earth. He is a prophetic seer who has had dreams and visions for many years. He was swimming in the river, and he was doing loop-de-loops in the water—like it was just his home. He was laughing and asked, "What took you so long?" as if he had been waiting for us. His face was beaming, fluorescent, and his arms were strong with big muscles. I remember seeing his right arm and his left arm, and both carried his body in the water as he was swimming all around.

Balls of Fire

As I was standing by this river, which came out of the sky, I saw an angel beside me who was throwing balls of fire into the rushing, gushing water. I looked behind me and saw many people swimming in the beautiful, crystal, sapphire, rushing, gushing river. As the balls of fire hit them, they screamed and fire came out of their mouths.

These were not bad screams, more like cleansing screams. I saw the fire in the midst of the gushing river burn away addictions and things that people had been crying about. The fire came and burnt them away. Then as the people swimming in the river got out of the river and began to talk, fire came out of their mouths. With every word they spoke, fire came out. I knew that the fire that proceeded from their mouths was a new authority coming on their spoken words.

As I turned and looked behind me again, I saw that the river had no boundaries. It had no limits. It spread to the north, to the south, to the east, and to the west—it touched everything. Everywhere behind me was shiny, crystal, sapphire, rushing, gushing water.

As I stepped into the beautiful, crystal, sapphire, gushing river, I again noticed the substance was soft, as if the water was oil, but it was water, and yet at the same time it was crystal—both smooth and soft. As I looked at the beautiful river, I let it run through my fingers.

I happened to look up and saw some men and women who had formed a circle and were standing at the door of a tent—all with wet clothes. Above the tent's door was a sign: Korah's Tent. I knew this was not good. I thought *How can anyone NOT be in this beautiful river?*

THE CLASSROOM

Then suddenly the scene of the dream changed, and I was in a school classroom. I was sitting in the front row of the class and there were many empty desks in the room. I looked up and saw that Jesus was the teacher. He had written the word *knowledge* five times on a large marker board, and He had a long, white stick. He was looking right at me, right into my eyes, and He turned and pointed at the words.

He had written the words like this on the marker board:

Knowledge Knowledge Knowledge

Knowledge Knowledge

He pointed His long, white stick at the board and pointed at each word and spoke that word out loud. He said, "Knowledge... knowledge..."

He said it five times and pointed at each word when He said it. As He spoke, He hit the marker board with His long, white stick.

Then He turned to look at me and He looked *into* me and *into* my eyes and said, "The heart is deceitfully wicked." Then He pointed at the words on the marker board again using His long, white stick. He said the words again, "Knowledge...knowledge..." five times, and then again He turned and looked right *into* my eyes and said again, "The heart is deceitfully wicked."

The heart is deceitful above all things and beyond cure. Who can understand it? I the LORD search the heart and examine the mind, to reward a man according to his conduct, according to what his deeds deserve (Jeremiah 17:9-10 NIV).

All of a sudden I was sitting with the Lord. It was as if we were *in the moment* of Matthew 5. He was speaking on the Beatitudes, and I was allowed to listen in. I felt as if I was taken by the hand of the Lord back in time to the very moment when Jesus was talking to His disciples about the Beatitudes.

THE BEATITUDES

We know that this passage of Scripture happened after Jesus had healed many, when the multitudes had begun following Him.

And seeing the multitudes, He went up on a mountain, and when He was seated His disciples came to Him (Matthew 5:1).

As I looked over this multitude of people, I noticed there were all social classes of people. When healing breaks out and Jesus Christ is healing, the multitudes follow. Every social and economic class comes; from the rich to the poor, those who are well bring those who are sick. Everyone comes when healing breaks out. Everyone comes when the river begins to flow.

When Jesus began to speak these beautiful words we call the Beatitudes, His eyes were landing upon the broken and pronouncing a blessing upon them. His eyes glanced over the multitude that was following Him and He began this great treasure of Scripture. The Word Himself opened His mouth and began to speak a blessing. The Word Himself opened His mouth and began to prophesy over the most broken of the broken. He was not simply saying that happy is the man who is poor, but the Word in the flesh was pronouncing a blessing.

Blessed are the poor in spirit, for theirs is the kingdom of heaven.

Blessed are those who mourn, for they shall be comforted.

Blessed are the meek, for they shall inherit the earth.

Blessed are those who hunger and thirst for righteousness, for they shall be filled.

Blessed are the merciful, for they shall obtain mercy.

Blessed are the pure in heart, for they shall see God.

Blessed are the peacemakers, for they shall be called sons of God.

Blessed are those who are persecuted for righteousness' sake, for theirs is the kingdom of heaven (Matthew 5:3-10).

I was sitting there in total amazement that I was even there watching all of this. It was like I was right there back in time. Jesus took a stroll back in time and He took my hand and brought me alongside Him as He spoke.

Then all of a sudden in the middle of this great blessing, He was speaking to me and giving me homework. As He began to speak the Beatitudes, He looked at me and said, "Go seek out the Greek meaning." And then He turned back and kept speaking to the crowd.

Now, I was me in this dream, and I was totally aware that I was me and that Jesus Himself was giving me a lesson on the Beatitudes.

BACK IN THE CLASSROOM

The dream scene shifted. I was back in the classroom study-ing the Beatitudes—looking up the Greek words. It was like I was really in class and every once in a while Jesus would walk by my desk and glance at my paper, as I did not have a computer but a paper and pencil. He was checking my work, and He would nod. I knew He really wanted me to understand this.

In my studies, I found that *blessed* means "happy." This *happy* is not merely being comfortable or entertained at the moment, it is "that joy which is completely independent of all the chances and changes of life."[1] Also, the verb *blessed* means to pronounce one blessed.[2]

Jesus, by the word of His mouth, was pronouncing a blessing and declaring, "You are not simply poor, you are blessed." His promise: *yours is the kingdom of heaven.*

Everyone can start here; it isn't first blessed are the pure
or the holy or the spiritual or the wonderful. Everyone
can be *poor in spirit*. "Not what I have, but what I have
not, is the first point of contact, between my soul and
God" (Spurgeon).[3]

His promise is given to the poor, the despised publicans, the
prostitutes, and those who are so poor they know they can offer
nothing and do not try. They cry for mercy and they alone are heard.
"The poor in spirit are lifted from the dunghill, and set, not among
hired servants in the field, but among princes in the kingdom...."[4]

In my dream, I was studying each word, each sentence, and
asking for the Spirit of Revelation. I desired to know and experience His heart more, that compassion would arise to a new level
and new height in my heart, that I would look like Jesus, talk like
Jesus, walk like Jesus, heal like Jesus, and live like Jesus.

WITH DAVID

Then the dream switched again, and I was taken back to the
time of David. I was watching David, and I could look *into* him
and see a wrestling on the inside of him. I saw him wrestling with
how he was treated as a younger brother. I saw him wrestling with
his thoughts and his emotions. He was wrestling with anger and
feeling as if he was being left out of things.

I saw that in the midst of watching over the sheep on the back
hills of Bethlehem during his youth, David struggled with his emotions and hurts. He was the youngest son. He was overlooked. He
was made fun of. He was given the lowest job.

I saw in *those* places he was wrestling on the inside with His
thoughts and emotions, and He was fighting even in his youth to
have right and correct thoughts about God. This struggle actually

catapulted him into the emotions of God. When David felt that no one else loved him, then *David knew God loved him.*

But the key is that this struggle of David's thoughts was actually moving God's heart. It was pleasing to God that David was battling in his mind, which was actually moving David's heart straight into God's heart.

This struggle was not wrong; it was good. I felt as if I was there when David was actually writing Psalm 19. Out of his wrestling this Psalm was birthed.

I saw David was realizing how *big* God is and how *small* he was. In Psalm 19 he wrote about the beauty of creation and the glory of God in the midst of all creation. David was trying to set his mind to *think of the greatness of God* right in the middle of the thoughts he was having and how he was being treated as a younger brother. David had struggled with his thoughts and emotions all night long. He was in the midst of describing the glory of God through creation when morning came and the sun began to break the dawn. All of a sudden, David looked up to see the sun arising in all of its strength.

David blurted out:

> *Who can discern his errors? Forgive my hidden faults. Keep your servant also from willful sins; may they not rule over me. Then I will be blameless, innocent of great transgression. May the words of my mouth and the meditation of my heart be pleasing in Your sight, O LORD, my Rock and my Redeemer* (Psalm 19:12-14 NIV).

I believe David was wrestling and groaning when he wrote this, fighting to keep his heart right with God and not become bitter.

As I began to slowly awake from this encounter with the Lord, I could see again the glorious river straight from the throne of God. Many leaders and many people were enjoying this river of

God, this beautiful Ezekiel 47 river coming from God's throne—and many people were having no struggle at all with it.

KORAH'S TENT

But, I also saw some people at the door of Korah's tent.

We find Korah in Numbers 16. Korah became jealous of Moses and Aaron, and he rose up against them along with 250 men of renown. Korah was the ring leader; he was a cousin to Moses. The men of renown were men of distinction and quality.[5]

In my dream, I saw two different kinds of leaders at the door of Korah's tent. But the key for both types is that God wants everybody to get *into* or *back into* the river. Our Father is always about restoration.

One group is struggling because they don't *feel* touched by the Spirit like other leaders. They are doing all they know to do to keep their thoughts right with God. They are in the midst of the great wrestle.

But because of this wrestle, the enemy is coming in like a flood and telling them they are getting overlooked because of jealousy. The enemy is shooting the fiery arrows of Ephesians 6 at them non-stop. He speaks to them like this: "I'm getting overlooked. No one likes me..." These are not even their own thoughts; the enemy is speaking to them in the first person and they are wrestling and wrestling.

When the enemy says, "You are overlooked. No one likes you," then they respond, "God blesses me. I am loved by God. God loves me...."

But then the enemy speaks into their thoughts, "No, God loves other people more than me. Look how I am always left out. I never get noticed. How come I can't be on stage? How come I don't feel the touch of the Spirit of the Lord like other people?"

Then they begin to wrestle again and say, "No, God blesses me. God loves me."

These thoughts and accusations are from the enemy. When they wrestle with these thoughts, it moves God's heart and moves them toward God. God is not angry. God loves this wrestle. This wrestle is one of the reasons that God picked David and said, "He is a man after My own heart."

Wrestling

Some of these leaders in this first group feel disqualified because of the wrestle, but the wrestle is actually going to thrust them into the depths of the river.

So in the dream I started yelling at them, "Keep fighting... keep wrestling...this is a good fight! This is a good wrestle that will lead to revelation of the emotions of God, just like it did with David!"

I kept yelling, "Keep wrestling...you are not disqualified. You feel overlooked and forgotten, but at the same time you are wrestling and fighting to find God in the midst of these fiery arrows and lies. He is pleased with you!

"HE IS COMING TO YOU!

"HE IS PLEASED WITH YOU!"

This first group of people needs to know that God is pleased with the wrestle and that they are *not* to give up because God is coming to them. Their wrestle will actually bring a blessing just like it brought to Jacob.

The Disgruntled Ones

The second group of people at Korah's tent is those who have always been the disgruntled ones. They have said, "I love the lowest place," but they only like the lowest place as long as they are never there.

This group is actually giving in to the fiery arrows. What is being written on their hearts is bitterness and resentment at the river and who the river is touching and who gets the microphone at different meetings and who gets to speak.

This group needs the fire. I started yelling at them, "Repent, lest you miss your visitation!" Some of them began to wrestle with their thoughts, and others became more offended and walked away from the beautiful, rushing, gushing river.

I looked up and I saw Heaven peering and watching. Faces were peering from the clouds, watching, suspenseful.

God's up to something and Heaven is watching.

As I awoke from this dream, I knew that God was after the first group with all passion. They have taken themselves out of the river because of the thoughts that they are wrestling with. The knowledge Jesus wants to impart to them—to you and me—is: *the struggle and the wrestle is actually drawing you closer to God.* God is not over-looking people because of the struggle of thoughts such as these:

- Why not me?
- Why can't I go on stage?
- Why am I not being noticed?
- Why can't I have favor?
- Why can't I be first?

In the midst of the dream I seemed to be watching a movie of the heart, and Jesus wanted me to understand that the thoughts that come from the enemy and the wrestle of our emotions to keep our heart right with God actually move the heart of God.

I believe a literal picture of this wrestling is when Jacob was wrestling with the angel of the Lord in Genesis 32:26. Then the man said, *"Let Me go, for the day breaks."* But Jacob replied, *"I will not let You go unless You bless me!"* This is the divine wrestle when we are wrestling with our thoughts, and our hearts just don't let go.

Keep Wrestling

Every time I read in the Book of Acts where James was killed, my heart goes out to John the Beloved. I think this was a wrestle moment for him. These two brothers did everything together. I think John wrestled with his emotions after James' death. I think John wrestled each time one of his friends was martyred, but that wrestle led him straight to the heart of God and straight into the vision of the Book of Revelation.

The Lord says, "Keep wrestling because the wrestle will lead you right to great revelation…and that wrestle will lead you straight to freedom and to joy! Just stay in the river."

Stay in the River

I invite everyone to stay in the river. You may be feeling over-looked or left out, but just stay in the river. It will bring healing to the mind and to the soul and bring life to all of the dry places in your life. Don't get out and don't get offended. God is watching and inviting you to let these living waters touch, heal, and renew your heart and your mind.

I believe that Jesus wrote the word *knowledge* on the marker board five times because we are in a season of grace to not only have knowledge about who He is but to personally experience Him.

I have not stopped giving thanks to God for you. I remember you in my prayers and ask the God of our Lord Jesus Christ, the glorious Father, to give you the Spirit, who will make you wise and reveal God to you, so that you will know Him. I ask that your minds may be opened to see His light, so that you will know what is the hope to which He has called you, how rich are the wonderful blessings He promises His people, and how very great is His power at work in us who believe. This power working in us is the same as the mighty strength which He used when He raised Christ from death and seated Him at His right side in the heavenly world (Ephesians 1:16-20 TEV).

Oh, that we would know Jesus Christ thoroughly. Oh, that we would understand His heart accurately, that we would recognize Him by sight, by hearing what He is saying, for His sheep hear His voice, that we would understand who Jesus is. The invitation He is giving us to understand Him and His heart is to stay in the river and to live, pray, and walk in the Beatitudes.

I invite you to go on a journey through the Beatitudes. Study the Greek meanings and mediate on the words that the Word Himself declared by the word of His mouth—He is commanding a blessing.

THE KINGDOM OF HEAVEN

"Blessed are the poor in spirit, for theirs is the kingdom of heaven" (Matt. 5:3).

Using definitions from *Strong's*, we can expand this to say: Blessed are those who are reduced to beggary, asking for alms, destitute of wealth, destitute of influence, position, honor, lowly, afflicted, helpless, powerless to accomplish an end. Blessed are those who are poor and needy, for theirs is the royal power, the kingship, the dominion, the right to rule, or the authority to rule, over a kingdom, over His Kingdom, the Kingdom of Heaven.

You're blessed when you're at the end of your rope. With less of you there is more of God and His rule (Matthew 5:3 TM).

They receive the kingdom of heaven because poverty of spirit is an absolute prerequisite for receiving the kingdom of heaven and as long as we harbor illusions about our own spiritual resources we will never receive from God what we absolutely need to be saved.[6]

"Blessed are those who mourn, for they shall be comforted" (Matt. 5:4).

Blessed are those who grieve and wail, for they shall be called near. They shall be invited near and in this nearness, they shall find comfort. The Lord is saying, "Blessed are you who mourn, for I will call you near; I will invite you near; I will console you."

> The Greek word for *mourn*, used here, is the strongest word for mourning in the Greek language. It is the word which is used for mourning for the dead, for the passionate lament for one who was loved.[7]

"Blessed are the meek, for they shall inherit the earth" (Matt. 5:5).

Blessed are the humble. Blessed are the gentle, for they shall receive as an inheritance the earth as a whole; they shall receive the portion assigned to them. They shall receive it as their own or as a possession to become partaker of; they shall obtain the inhabited earth, the abode of men and animals, a country; they shall receive the land enclosed within fixed boundaries, a tract of land, territory, region.

> The meek person was not passive or easily pushed around. The main idea behind the word "meek" was strength under control, like a strong stallion that was trained to do the job instead of running wild.[8]

Meek also refers to "the men who suffer wrong without bitterness or desire for revenge."[9]

"Blessed are those who hunger and thirst for righteousness, for they shall be filled" (Matt. 5:6).

Blessed are those who are famished. Blessed are those who are thirsty. Blessed are those who crave innocence. Blessed are those who are not just a little bit hungry, for they shall have righteousness in abundance. They shall gorge on holiness and be satisfied. They shall be filled up and satisfied with righteousness.

"Blessed are the merciful, for they shall obtain mercy" (Matt. 5:7).

Blessed are the compassionate. Blessed are those who are actively compassionate, for they shall obtain compassion. They shall obtain human mercy and divine mercy.

"Blessed are the pure in heart, for they shall see God" (Matt. 5:8).

Blessed are those who are clean. Blessed are those who are clear, who are pure in their thoughts or feelings. Blessed are those who are clean in their hearts and in their minds, for they shall gaze with wide-open eyes; they shall appear; they shall see God. Blessed are those whose actions and thoughts are pure, for they shall appear before God.

This *is* the cry of David: "Let the words of my heart and the mediation of my mind be acceptable in Your sight. May everything I think about be pleasing to You, God" (see Ps. 19:14).

"Blessed are the peacemakers, for they shall be called sons of God" (Matt. 5:9).

Blessed are the mediators. Blessed are those who try to make peace by reconciling parties who disagree or quarrel or fight, for their names shall be sons of God.

"Blessed are those who are persecuted for righteousness' sake, for theirs is the kingdom of heaven" (Matt. 5:10).

Blessed are those who are pursued with harassing or oppressive treatment because of religion, race, or beliefs. Blessed are those who are troubled persistently because they are innocent or righteous. Blessed are those who are harassed for the sake of righteousness, for theirs is the rule; theirs is the mountain where God dwells; theirs is the realm of Heaven.

> *Blessed are you when they revile and persecute you, and say all kinds of evil against you falsely for My sake. Rejoice and be exceedingly glad, for great is your reward in heaven, for so they persecuted the prophets who were before you* (Matthew 5:11-12).

Blessed are you when you are taunted or assailed with contemptuous or opprobrious language. Blessed are you when others address, speak abusively, defame, or literally pursue or follow you and bring a false word against you. Blessed are you when everything they say is vicious and full of malice, or grievous and harmful, wicked, lewd, and false. Blessed are you when people lie concerning you on account of Me. I say be cheerful, be happy, be exceedingly glad, be joyful, and jump for joy. Have exceeding joy and rejoice greatly for great are the rewards that God bestows, that God gives in Heaven, the consummately perfect place where God dwells. For they persecuted the men filled with the Spirit of God, who by God's authority and command in words of weight pleaded the cause of God and urged the salvation of men. They also persecuted these who went before you.

ENDNOTES

1. William Barclay, quoted by David Guzik, Enduring Word Media, 2010. http://enduringword.com/commentaries/4005.htm (accessed November 5, 2010).
2. *Strong's Exhaustive Concordance*, KJV New Testament Greek Lexicon, electronic edition. http://www.biblestudytools.com/concordances/strongs-exhaustive-concordance/
3. Guzik, http://enduringword.com/commentaries/4005.htm
4. Charles Spurgeon, quoted by Guzik. http://enduringword.com/commentaries/4005.htm

5. Biblesoft PC Bible Study version 5.0 (2007).
6. Guzik. http://enduringword.com/commentaries/4005.htm
7. William Barclay, quoted by Guzik. http://enduringword.com/commentaries/4005.htm
8. Guzik. http://enduringword.com/commentaries/4005.htm
9. F.F. Bruce, quoted by Guzik. http://enduringword.com/commentaries/4005.htm

Chapter 31

The Watchmen and the Wise

*Those who are wise will shine like the brightness of the heavens, and
those who lead many to righteousness, like the stars forever and ever*
(Daniel 12:3 NIV).

I had a dream. I was getting off a train in Poland. It was cold
out and I had my winter coat on. It was wet and to the natural eye
seemed dreary. It must have been in the late evening as I remember
stepping off of the train and the glimmering stars got my attention. They were shining so brightly, and in the midst of darkness
their lights were even brighter. I did not even notice how dark it
was because the lights were so bright in the sky.

The cool air began to blow on my face and on my ears, so I pulled my coat collar up to break the wind. In that moment, I thought I heard whispers in the wind. It was like the angels and the great host of Heaven were peering into this small nation. I kept hearing whispers, "The house of the watchmen and the wise; I am raising up My house of the watchmen and the wise."

I noticed a lot of trains in the land, and these trains were running quickly down the tracks. I kept watching these large locomotives. A loud horn coming from the engine announced to everyone that "this train is moving forward." I saw the wheels begin to turn, slowly at first, then gradually picking up speed to race down the tracks with deafening speed and sound. The mechanical force behind the trains was so strong that mere mortals could never stand in front of them and stop them.

GOD'S HOUSE

As I watched the trains race down the tracks, I kept hearing the word *acceleration.* I believe God is bringing a great acceleration to His house of the watchmen and the wise in Poland. He is stirring the hearts of His watchmen in Poland and raising up His house, filling it with those who are crying out for His purposes and also those who are wise.

God's house is going to progress like a train. It is going to start off slowly but will build momentum and then lift up a sound that mere mortals cannot stop. God is drawing the hearts of those who have oil in their lamps. These are the ones who have given themselves to countless hours in prayer when no one was looking, and their lamps are filled to the brim with oil. These are the ones who do not just know the Word but also know the yearnings of the heart of God. Their histories in God are shining forth like lights in the dead of night.

God is raising up His house of prayer in Poland, and just as the trains reach the farthest parts of the land, so will His house extend to every corner. To the north, south, east, and west, there is a sound arising as God is raising up the house of the watchmen and the wise in the land of Poland. He is setting His watchmen on the wall to cry out day and night, and they will shine like the brightness of Heaven. They do not fear darkness; it is only a reminder that the wise of the land are being set in place by the hand of the Lord.

I remember watching a train slowly begin its journey down the tracks and I thought, *I will remember this train and its movements down the tracks. It will remind me that You, O God, are sitting Your house in place in Poland and it will look just like this train—starting off slowly with a loud horn, a loud sound and roar. It will pick up momentum with every prayer and every song until it is an unstoppable force in the land of Poland.*

I began to walk the land. It was as if I was really there for I remember the feeling of each step as I began my journey—each step was a giant one, so I could walk the width of the land in a short amount of time. It seemed I was 30 feet tall and looking down upon this land. I heard the Lord say, "I am letting you see the land from My view—this is what I see." I saw many A-frame houses and cottages with the lights on inside. I got up close and looked in the windows of a few. I saw people gathered in living rooms sitting in a circle and praying. Their Bibles were opened to Colossians I, and they were praying this passage over their districts.

For this reason we also, since the day we heard it, do not cease to pray for you, and to ask that you may be filled with the knowledge of His will in all wisdom and spiritual understanding; that you may walk worthy of the Lord, fully pleasing Him, being fruitful in every good work and increasing in the knowledge of God; strengthened with all might, according to His glorious power, for all patience and longsuffering with joy; giving thanks to the Father who has qualified us to be partakers of the inheritance of the saints in the light.

He has delivered us from the power of darkness and conveyed us into the kingdom of the Son of His love, in whom we have redemption through His blood, the forgiveness of sins.

He is the image of the invisible God, the firstborn over all creation (Colossians 1:9-15).

At first what I saw seemed to be simple prayer meetings. But what got my attention was the roof of each of these A-frame houses and cottages. As worship arose and as the prayers within the homes reached the roofs, they began to burn with fire. When the wind blew, it stirred up the flames on the top of the houses and they scattered all over the land.

People outside noticed the flames burning on the roofs, yet the fire did not burn down the houses. The sign of the Spirit of the Lord was resting upon each home where the incense of prayer and worship was arising. One by one people outside began knocking on the doors and asking, "Can I come in? What are you doing? Can I pray too? I need God. I need a Savior."

What seemed difficult before was now easy—as people lifted their voices in prayer, the sound rose to the throne of God. God gazed upon the cottages of prayer and worship and breathed a fire that does not consume wood, hay, and stubble—a fire that turns the hearts of men and women.

God Is Listening!

I was so excited. I began to run through the land yelling, "God is listening! God is watching you, Poland. You are in His gaze. Keep praying. Keep worshiping. Don't stop!"

Then, just as the dream began, there I was again, standing at the train station watching a train begin to move forward. I could feel a cold breeze on my face and again I could hear the whispers in the wind, "The house of the watchmen and the wise, I am raising up My house of the watchmen and the wise." I had renewed hope of what God was doing in Poland. I saw with my own eyes God raising up His house of the watchmen and the wise. I saw the Spirit of God like fire resting upon the frame of each cottage where His people were singing and praying. I saw the Lord begin to stir the hearts of the lost in the land, one by one and soul by soul, that they too would lift up a cry for God's purposes in the land of Poland.

Let me encourage you—dreams have many layers, and though I saw this dream for Poland, it is a dream that we can pray over every nation, as we see only in part. God is raising up His house of the watchmen and the wise from nation to nation. So join with many who cry out to see watchmen set on the wall in many cities, in many nations. Let these watchmen never stop crying out, day and night.

I have set watchmen on your walls, O Jerusalem; they shall never hold their peace day or night. You who make mention of the LORD, do not keep silent (Isaiah 62:6).

Chapter 32

When the Lamb Stands

Then I looked, and I heard the voice of many angels around the throne, the living creatures, and the elders; and the number of them was ten thousand times ten thousand, and thousands of thousands, saying with a loud voice: "Worthy is the Lamb who was slain to receive power and riches and wisdom, and strength and honor and glory and blessing!" (Revelation 5:11-12)

I had a dream. I was walking through multitudes and multitudes of people. Everyone was standing and singing. I saw many, many bodies of people looking straight ahead and singing with voices that resonated. When I looked up, I could see the vibrations of the sound as their voices went forth. The vibrations looked like arrows going forth with a purpose. The beautiful harmonies and tones and sounds penetrated to the core of my heart.

I asked myself, *Where am I?* It was as if suddenly I had been transported to a place that was so beautiful, so peaceful, and so filled with perfection. Life was in the air; beauty was in the air. My spirit knew exactly where I was, but my mind and body needed some time to catch up. I looked around trying to figure out where I was, as every part of my mind, soul, and heart was filled with peace and love.

The sound of the voices was powerful; the song was being sung with many voices but they sounded as one voice. I kept hearing, "Worthy...worthy...worthy is the Lamb who was slain. Worthy...worthy...worthy is the Lamb who was slain." I heard it over and over and over like waves in a constant motion of glory.

When I looked down at my feet, I saw I was walking on a blue pavement—but it was not pavement. There was firmness to it, yet it was soft like gel. I looked more closely, and as I bent down to touch the blue surface, I noticed that it was not ground at all—it was water. I knew then where I was.

The Great Crystal Sea

I was standing right inside Revelation chapters 4 and 5. I love this place. It is so beautiful. It is thunderous. It is glorious. It is joyful. It is peaceful. There is no "high" like the high that the spirit feels when standing in the presence of God and the glorious Lamb.

I was standing on the great crystal sea, yet this time I was not alone. The great crystal sea was filled with people, voices, sounds, songs, words, vibrations, and rhythms. I could hear the roar of the sea, and everyone and everything was worshiping God on the throne and the Lamb. All of Heaven knows the eternal, the immortal God and the Lamb. Every part of everything created in the heavens sing out a song of worship to the One who sits upon the throne and to the glorious Lamb.

I heard the Spirit of the Lord in the depths of me say, "Come as close as you want. Come as close as you want. Come as close as you want." He was beckoning me to come closer and closer. I wanted to get as close to the front as I could. I wanted to see up close. I wanted to hear up close.

As I walked through the great cloud of people, I thought, *I am stepping on the crystal sea in the midst of multitudes of people. There are so many voices that it sounds like musical thunder all praising God on the throne and the Lamb. Here I am—in the great tabernacle of meeting right on the crystal sea.* I could see Jesus Christ Himself standing and all of Heaven giving glory to the slain One. Songs were rising, "Oh the beautiful Lamb who was slain and with His own blood He purchased men for God."

I pushed toward the front, and suddenly there I was. It was just as beautiful as it was the first time—for I have been to this place once before and have stood on the crystal sea. The previous time I was permitted to peer into the worship service of Heaven from Revelation 4, but this time I could see the Lamb—this time I was allowed closer and closer. I believe God wanted me to see, experience, and touch what Heaven looked like. My Father had bid me to come closer and closer—I was going to go.

GOLDEN LAMP STANDS

I walked right into the midst of the golden lamp stands. They were real. I could touch them. They were gigantic. They were golden. Everything was big. Written at the base of every lamp stand were the letters to the seven churches. As I walked past the first, it actually spoke to me, "Remember your First Love." As I heard those words, they ignited inside of me—*remember your First Love.*

A new passion rose up in me at the hearing of those words. As I kept walking, each lamp stand bent over and spoke to my heart. These were real lamp stands with torches of light that penetrated into my mind and heart. Everything in Heaven has life in it, and everything has an understanding of the cost of the Lamb of God who laid down His life willingly for all humankind.

As I kept walking among the stands, each one whispered into my right ear: remember your First Love; be faithful unto death; repent; hold fast what you have till I come; be watchful; strengthen what remains; I know your works—I have set before you an open door; buy from Me gold refined by fire.

I heard these words coming from the different lamp stands, and I could read the letters that were engraved in the base of the lamp stands. These phrases were like whispers in the wind that I kept hearing over and over and over. Heaven is beckoning the hearts of humankind back to the days when John received this revelation the first time. I felt strengthened in my spirit as I heard the whispers. *Remember... Be faithful... Repent... Hold fast... Be watchful... Strengthen... I know your works... Buy gold....*

I knew that these words and these letters written so long ago were words of life for the human soul in our day. For these words written in years past had meaning and revelation that were prodding my heart to walk them out in these days.

THE LIVING CREATURES

I continued to walk closer and closer to the throne. Then I came upon and saw the living creatures. It was as if every movement of their beings was reaching for the throne of God. There was passion in every single one of their movements. From the gaze of their eyes to the tip of their wings—up and down and down and up—everything was extended as if trying to touch the throne of God and the Lamb. They were not tired. They were not weary. Every movement was stretched out—the tips of their wings pointed directly to the throne as if trying to get as close as possible to touch Him—pure beauty and pure glory.

I looked up and saw the rainbow that encircled the throne of God. It was radiant, and the words *mercy, mercy, mercy, mercy* came out of its color as if the rainbow itself had a voice. It was as if the rainbow itself was alive and had its own song of mercy to sing around the great throne of God. Everything circles the great throne and the Lamb. Everything points to it. Everyone is gazing on it—to Him who sits on the throne and unto the Lamb.

Oh, the beauty of the Lamb.

When the Lamb stands, it is a beautiful sight. There is knowledge in Heaven of what the Lamb has done—the knowledge of His love, His righteousness, His beauty, His perfection, His glory, His reign, and His blood.

In unison, the whole multitude standing on the crystal sea fell down, along with the elders, and cast their golden crowns to the ground.

And the sounds came forth:

WORTHY IS THE LAMB.

WORTHY IS THE LAMB.

TO HIM BE ALL POWER AND RICHES AND WISDOM AND STRENGTH AND HONOR AND BLESSING AND GLORY!

It was like a hurricane in the midst of the throne. All people, creatures, and angels, sang it again and again—worthy is the Lamb!

INTO WORSHIP AND PRAYER

Then suddenly, the dream switched and in an instant I was walking *in the midst* of the worship and prayer movement. I was walking down the aisle, and I heard those on earth singing this same song with the same passion—the voices were as one singing to Him who sits on the throne and to the Lamb of God.

Blessing and glory, honor and power be to the Lamb forever and ever. Those words were sung over and over with great passion, with beautiful harmonies, with the sounds of many loud voices and tones and vibrations being sung to the Lamb on the throne—yet I was on earth.

I was walking up and down an aisle and people everywhere on earth were singing the same song that I heard in eternity. I walked past a group of dancers and they themselves *looked* like the living creatures. The way they danced—each finger pointing upward, no movement lost or done half-heartedly—looked like what I had just seen in eternity. Every part of their bodies, from their fingers to their faces and eyes and the movement of their feet, were all pointing to the throne of God and to the Lamb.

INTO HEAVEN

Then in an instant, I was transported again into Heaven, and was watching those standing on the crystal sea as they sang and bowed. I was watching the living creatures gently and in perfect motion encircle the throne where no movement was lost—everything that is done in Heaven points to God and to the Lamb. No song is lost, no phrase cut short or sung half-heartedly. Each word and each note was sung with passion, adoration, and love—a sound that is all-consuming.

It was as if I was going back and forth. I was seeing and experiencing the worship in Heaven, watching the great cloud of witnesses standing on the crystal sea, and hearing the voices that God hears encircling His great throne. I knew He wanted me to hear the voices that surround the Lamb when all Heaven bows low and gives Him glory. Then I was brought back to earth to hear the sound of those worshiping with all of their hearts *on earth.* I went back and forth to the worship in Heaven and then to the worship on earth.

Suddenly I looked up, and Jesus was looking at me. The Lamb spoke to me, "Worship and prayer on the earth is starting to look just like Heaven looks. It is beginning to sound just like Heaven sounds."

The Lamb was smiling, and He was taking large deep breaths as if He wanted to breathe in every note of every song that was being sung. For on the earth our praises arise like sweet incense, and He loves our voices. He loves our sounds. He hears everything, and Heaven is aware of the worship and prayer on the earth—it is beginning to sound like Heaven. We are beginning to sing one song to Him who sits on the throne and unto the glorious Lamb of God.

> *...Let me see your face, let me hear your voice; for your voice is sweet, and your face is lovely* (Song of Solomon 2:14).

Chapter 33

Stand Firm

After you have done everything, stand.
Stand firm then, Iceland.
Stand firm then, America.
Stand firm then, New Zealand.

In this dream, I saw a picture of what Ephesians 6 really looks like. Paul admonished the Ephesians to daily *"Put on the whole armor of God, that you may be able to stand against the wiles of the devil"* (Eph. 6:11).

We must do this also. These are real weapons that we wear, and we are fighting a real war against the powers of darkness. This is the day to *wake up* and put on our strength. We must loose ourselves from the bonds around our necks, for we are on the Lord's side and the host of Heaven is joining us in this battle—but we are the ones who must fight.

GREETINGS FROM ICELAND

I had a dream. I was sleeping in my bed and the house I was in was spinning and spinning, until suddenly, I was carried by this house to a faraway land. When I woke up, the sun was shining brightly, almost as if it never went down. I sat up in my bed and looked out the window. It was bright and sunny and green, and there were streams and waters and fountains and rivers flowing everywhere. I thought I was in Heaven again for it was so beautiful.

The landscape was stunning. The grass was the greenest of green and it seemed to melt right into the blue of the sky. The grass fit the landscape so well, and it was so green, that it almost appeared unreal.

I went outside to get a better view of this stunning picture. It was like a dream because it was so beautiful and the colors were so vivid that they did not even look real.

In the distance I saw a man walking toward me. He was not in a hurry but seemed to be taking in the same beauty that I was enjoying. I felt like I was in a movie because he was walking toward me almost in slow motion and was fully dressed as a warrior. As he approached me, he said, "Greetings from the land of Iceland."

I was totally shocked, so I repeated his statement with a question, "Greetings from the land of Iceland? This is Iceland?" I expected Iceland to be cold and full of ice. I was unprepared for my eyes to see such beauty. For the colors of the sky were those of many colors. The sea was a picture in itself, and when I looked into the distance to where the sea met the sky, it was like I was looking into a prism—the light throughout the sky separated into a spectrum of fantastic colors I had never seen before—a unique rainbow sky.

A HEAVENLY WARRIOR

Then I began to study this man who was standing before me dressed as a warrior, as if he came fully prepared to go to war on the frontlines. I noticed a thick, wide belt that had the word **TRUTH** in bold, black capital letters written across the buckle. Across the front of his chest was a glimmering breastplate. I remember thinking that nothing would be able to penetrate that breastplate because of its thickness. It covered his whole chest, and written on the front, also in black, bold capital letters, was the word **RIGHTEOUSNESS**.

Instantly my eyes were opened to the fact that I was looking at a heavenly warrior dressed in the whole armor of God. He looked like what Paul wrote about to the Ephesian believers in Ephesians 6. This is the armor that will lead to victory when fighting battles on the earth. As I leaned in closer I saw that this Heavenly Warrior was not just any angel within the host of Heaven but was the Captain of the hosts Himself. His very walk seemed to bring peace—security, safety, prosperity, joy, and harmony—in His steps. He was the very embodiment of walking in the gospel of peace. In His left hand He carried a shield of faith that no flaming arrows would dare penetrate. His armor showed the wear of many battles, but His walk was one of strength and steadiness.

In His right hand was a sword that looked larger than my whole body. He carried it with ease and readiness as the Word of God came forth out of His mouth with authority and boldness. He knew who He was and whom He was fighting for; He was from the camp of the Lord God Jehovah. Covering and guarding His head was a helmet, which I knew was the helmet of salvation for He brought with Him the very hope of salvation.

He looked into my eyes and said, "Prophesy over the land for the hearts of the people are becoming weary. For witchcraft and the spirit of the age are quickly capturing the hearts of the young and old, and those who have been calling on the name of the Lord have become weary."

He turned and shouted, "You shall live again, Iceland! You shall live again." He said, "Call to the hearts of the people." Then He shouted Ephesians 6:10-18 (NIV) into the land:

Be strong in the Lord and in His mighty power.

*Put on the full armor of God so that you can take your stand against the devil's schemes. For our struggle is not against flesh and blood, but against the rulers, against the authorities, against the powers of this dark world and against the spiritual forces of evil in the heavenly realms. Therefore put on the full armor of God, so that when the day of evil comes, you may be able to stand your ground, and after you have done everything, to **stand**.*

***Stand firm** then, with the belt of truth buckled around your waist, with the breastplate of righteousness in place, and with your feet fitted with the readiness that comes from the gospel of peace. In addition to all this, take up the shield of faith, with which you can extinguish all the flaming arrows of the evil one. Take the helmet of salvation and the sword of the Spirit, which is the word of God. And pray in the Spirit on all occasions with all kinds of prayers and requests. . . .*

Suddenly I found myself clothed in the very armor He was clothed in. My eyes were opened in a new way to see the principalities and demons of darkness fighting for control over this land. And I began to fight in this great war of two realms as if I was in the movie *Lord of the Rings*. It was crazy! Clothed in this armor

I was almost untouchable, and I could see with my natural eyes the battle of darkness. I could see we were not fighting against mere physical opponents, but these were powers of darkness, master demonic spirits, world rulers of the darkness of this age, and spiritual forces of wickedness. These were real beings of evil that I could see affecting human minds and hearts in Iceland. There was only one way to fight this battle and win. I could hear the real sound of swords striking upon sword.

Darkness does not give up easily. It strikes and strikes at any areas not covered until the people are beaten down. I could see the great importance of wearing and using the whole armor of God.

JOINING THE BATTLE

I found myself joining this great battle against these real warriors. I had to step out in a new faith believing that God was my guard, for this was a battle I had not fought before. This was war; Light versus dark, holiness versus sin, heavenly versus demonic, Good versus evil. This was the real deal. I saw that the warlords of darkness were real and their plan was to break down the hearts of believers in the land one strike at a time. Knowing I fought beside the great Heavenly Warrior, I struck with my sword. At first I started swinging with my eyes closed, as it was just too much to take in—but at least I was swinging. I gained strength as I began singing in the Spirit. I used my shield of faith, and I became untouchable by the flaming arrows of darkness.

Suddenly, strike by strike, my eyes were opened and I saw that I could not be touched by the strategies of evil and the doctrines of demons. Then I heard the Captain of the Hosts Himself prophesy over the land:

Be strong in the Lord and in the power of His might.
Put on God's complete armor that you may be able to

resist and stand your ground on the evil day of danger and having done all to stand—stand therefore. Hold your ground!

So I began to shout it out too, "Be strong in the Lord and in the power of *His* might. Put on the whole armor of God. It works...it really works!"

Then I began to pray in the Spirit, with every strike of the sword of the Spirit against the enemies of Light. I began to sing in the Spirit, and as I sang, I saw my voice as a strike against the enemy as if I was loosing the army of God with every note and every prayer that proceeded from my mouth. My song became a weapon against the powers of darkness as much as my armor was a weapon and protection. With every note that I sang out in the Spirit, the forces of evil began to dissipate.

Suddenly, the sound of singing filled the land, and one by one people came out of hiding, came out of their caves, and began to strengthen themselves and fight. Soon there was a multitude on the Lord's side literally pushing back darkness and pushing back schemes and strategies of evil.

The One I was fighting with looked at me and spoke a command: "Prophesy over America. Prophesy over New Zealand in the same way, for My house is growing weary and it is time to fight."

In my mind, I was taken back to the days of King David. I saw a picture of King David in First Samuel 30. He was weary, for it seemed that all was stolen from him.

> Now it happened, when David and his men came to Ziklag, on the third day, that the Amalekites had invaded the South and Ziklag, attacked Ziklag and burned it with fire, and had taken captive the women and those who were there, from small to great; they did not kill anyone, but carried them away and went their way. So David and his men came to the city, and there it was, burned with fire; and

their wives, their sons, and their daughters had been taken captive. Then David and the people who were with him lifted up their voices and wept, until they had no more power to weep.

...But David strengthened himself in the LORD his God....

*So David inquired of the LORD, saying, "Shall I pursue this troop? Shall I overtake them?" And He answered him, "Pursue, for you shall surely overtake them and without fail **recover** all"* (I Samuel 30:1-4,6,8).

Then in the dream I began to call Iceland to put on the full armor of God and "pursue, for you shall surely overtake and without fail recover all."

I began to call to the United States of America to "pursue, for you will surely overtake and without fail recover all."

And I began to call forth New Zealand to "pursue, for you will surely overtake and without fail recover all."

This is a battle. This is a war with real warlords of darkness, and they are fighting to win. They do not take breaks, and they do not give up. But we have a greater weapon—the blood of the Lamb. Because of His blood we can:

- Be strong in the Lord and in the power of His might.
- Put on God's complete armor.
- Resist and stand our ground on the evil day of danger.
- Stand and hold our ground.

Chapter 34

Gotta Get Higher

My son, give attention to my words; incline your ear to my sayings. Do not let them depart from your eyes; keep them in the midst of your heart; for they are life to those who find them, and health to all their flesh. Keep your heart with all diligence, for out of it spring the issues of life. Put away from you a deceitful mouth, and put perverse lips far from you. Let your eyes look straight ahead, and your eyelids look right before you. Ponder the path of your feet, and let all your ways be established. Do not turn to the right or the left; remove your foot from evil (Proverbs 4:20-27).

On a Thursday night during one of our renewal services in Kansas City, I heard the voice of the Lord in the depths of me say, "Get to the front. Get to the front." I heard the Lord say, "When you get to the front, someone is going to pray for you, and when they do, give yourself to it."

So I started heading toward the front but was hindered by many people wanting prayer. I stopped and prayed over them. Yet still inside I could hear the voice of the Lord shouting, "Get to the front!" So I headed toward the front of the prayer line. I felt someone touch my left arm. I looked up and saw one of our pastors. His eyes were glazed over, and he said, "I'm going to pray for you."

I closed my eyes and I felt my legs become like Jell-O. I remember hearing his voice as he began to pray for me, but I don't remember words. My legs would not work. I could not hold myself up. I went down.

As my body fell to the floor, about 30 seconds later I felt someone grab my wrists. I opened my eyes to see two large angels on either side of me picking me up by my wrists. They were saying over and over, "Gotta get higher. Gotta get higher. Gotta get higher."

ANGEL WINGS

I could hear their wings fluttering faster and faster as if they were trying with all of their strength to get me higher. I looked up and saw an open portal, an open heaven right in the center of the building. I could see a beautiful, blue expanse right beyond the top of the building, and I wanted to get through it. I was so excited to be escorted by angels who were saying to me, "You have to get higher."

I could see with my eyes that the open portal was our destination—for there was a real opening and these angels were trying with all of their might to get me higher—but I seemed to be dangling about five feet off the ground.

I looked down and I could see myself lying out in the spirit. I could see my body lying on the floor, but at the same time I was still about five feet off of the ground listening to the flutter of angel wings. They continued to say, "Gotta get higher. Gotta get higher. Gotta get higher." And still we did not move; we stayed in the same place.

I could see the whole meeting going on, but no one saw me in the air. They stepped over my body lying on the floor, but they could not see me dangling in the air—being held up by the two angels. What a sight it would have been for the human eye to see!

I saw two other angels carrying up another woman in our midst, and she was ascending quickly. She was like a slinky toy going up and down and up and down. And she was lit up as if a florescent lightbulb was shining out of her belly. She looked clean and shiny, like someone had scrubbed her up and down with soap. She was glowing and radiating. She went up through the small portal easily and then came back down.

I started praying, "Make me like a slinky, God, so that I can easily go up through that open heaven."

STUCK

But for some reason, I was stuck. I remained only five feet off the ground dangling in the air with the two angels holding me by my wrists, their wings fluttering faster and faster and faster. They continued to say, "Gotta get higher, gotta get higher, gotta get higher." But we were not moving at all. By this time, my arm joints were beginning to hurt. I was hanging by my wrists, and it was becoming uncomfortable.

I am not that heavy—I'm only 4' 11½". So I turned my head and said, "What's the problem? I'm not that heavy. You are angels. I thought angels were supposed to be strong, but you can't even lift me up."

Then all of a sudden I felt someone grab the back of my shirt by my collar and pick me up. I shot up 50 feet into the sky like I was on a carnival ride, and my stomach felt sick because it happened so quickly. I went right through the building roof, but it was like my body turned to air. All of a sudden I was looking straight into the face of a huge angel. He had his right arm on his waist and he was dangling me in the air by his left hand where he had grabbed the collar of my shirt.

Shut the Gates!

He looked into my eyes with great sternness and said, "It is not *them*, it is *you!* You have too many gates open—your eye gate, your ear gate, your mouth gate. What you watch, what you listen to, and what you say. This portal is very narrow, and you can only get through it with these worldly gates closed. *Shut the gates!* Hear me now. Let these gates be extremely guarded because what goes in will *always* come out."

He was face to face with me, but his face was so big—as big as my whole body. His skin was bronze. His voice was like thunder. His words like a strong wind. The sternness of his face made me want to hide. The breath coming from his mouth was blowing my whole body backward, and I could hardly breathe because the winds that came from His voice were as strong as a hurricane.

Suddenly I heard a loud, "BAM, BAM, BAM!" And I saw three large gates close.

Then he thundered at me again with his voice like the strength of a mighty wind, *"Keep them closed!"* His command resonated throughout every cell of my body like thunder going through a valley that rolls and rolls and echoes far in the distance. His voice rumbled, *"Shut the gates, keep them closed!"*

All of a sudden I went shooting up and in a split second I went through an open portal in the sky right over the Forerunner Christian Fellowship. It was a beautiful, blue opening. But this time I did not see a ladder; I just saw angels going and coming and coming and going and I heard the fluttering of wings. They were very busy. I heard the fluttering of wings everywhere.

HEAVEN

I saw many scenes at the same time. It was like I was doing and seeing everything at the same time. I saw faces in the great cloud of witnesses watching what was going on on earth. Everyone in Heaven is rejoicing with us. I saw so many familiar faces.

I saw one man running as fast as he could run, and he was jumping and leaping in the air and skipping. He was yelling, "This is exhilarating! This is exhilarating!" A woman said, "He has not stopped doing this since the day he got here," and she was laughing. I knew this man on earth, and he had been a quadriplegic for many years. Now in Heaven, he had legs and arms and a body that was whole and complete. He was running and skipping and leaping for he was in the presence of the fullness of joy.

I was placed at a table with lots of small brown books on the table. The books were about one inch long and thin. One of the angels that brought me up said, "Open up," and he began to stuff all of these little brown books into my mouth.

He said, "Chew it and eat it." Another angel was putting these small books into my head. And they kept saying, "The Word, the Word, the Word. You must be full of the Word." They said that over and over.

Then they grabbed me by my wrists again and started taking me higher. They put a veil over my face as it was getting brighter and brighter the more we ascended. I had to put my hands in front of the veil that was covering my eyes because the light was so bright, but they still held me by the wrists and took me higher. They kept saying, "Gotta get higher, gotta get higher. Gotta get higher."

Finally we stopped. They took the veil off of my face. I found myself looking into a big, black, round mass about 50 feet in circumference. I could not grasp what I was looking at. All I saw was a large circle of what seemed like a black mass, but I felt *longing* coming from the mass, like love was pulsing my very being and drawing me as near as I could fathom myself going. I felt my heart become exceedingly tender as love seemed to pierce the depths of my being. I was feeling all of this while looking at the black mass. I stepped back as I thought I was still in the air, but I was on a solid foundation. I gasped when I realized what I was seeing and how near I was to God—for I realized that I was looking right *into the eye of God*. Not eyes as in plural, but the *eye of God*.

THE EYE OF GOD

The black of the eye of God was a beautiful black, and it was pulsing, beckoning me to come as close as I wanted. The eye never blinked; it was focused directly on me. The angels that carried me by my wrists said, "Step inside."

So very slowly I began to step inside the pupil, the mass. I stepped inside the *longing*. I stepping inside the vibration of passion that seemed to be waiting just for me and bidding me to come as close as I wanted. I was not fearful. It was a feeling of complete love and acceptance. For He wanted me to come close to step inside His gaze just the way I was. I was not asked to leave and come back when I had my act together. I was not asked to come back another day when He had more time, for all His time was focused on me.

Ever so slowly, as if in slow motion, I stepped into the pupil of the eye of God.

What I saw left me in total amazement. For as I stepped into the pupil of His eye, I found myself. There I was right in the center of His gaze! Every second of every minute of my life, He held me close in the center of His pupil, and I did not even realize it until I saw myself sitting and resting in the pupil of the Almighty God.

And then, just for a second, I saw a multitude of believers also hidden and tucked away in the very pupil of His eye. In that precise second, I realized that we are not the apples *of* God's eye, but we are the apples *in* God's eye. We are *in* Him. We are in His gaze always!

As I looked around, I saw the depth of His pupil. It went on for miles and miles, for God never ends and His gaze reaches everywhere. There is room enough for everyone in the pupil of His eye. We are all there.

I could see a mental picture of Psalm 17 where King David says, *"Keep and guard me as the pupil of Your eye; hide me in the shadow of Your wings"* (Ps. 17:8 AMP).

We are in the pupil of the eye of God, the very center of His gaze. God has placed us in the center of His gaze and He never sleeps; we are always in His pupil. When you have something in your eye, you cannot forget that something is there, and we are in His pupil.

I just sat down right next to myself, sitting in the pupil of the eye of God. I began to mediate on the kindness of God that He would bring me this close and let me see with my eyes that He has always carried me this close.

I began to ponder how I got there and remembered the stern voice that said, "Shut the gates"—my eye gate, my ear gate, my mouth gate, that which I watch with my eyes and listen to and say with my mouth. I found myself praying and asking for help to keep these gates closed. I laid my head back and leaned against the One who watches over me and never sleeps and never slumbers—and in this place I rested.

He Leads Us in All Truth

Then, as quickly as this encounter started, it was over. I was back in my body. My husband was helping me off the floor. My shoulder joints were in pain as if my body had really been dangling in the air. I went and sat in a chair to let my mind recall all that my spirit had experienced. I kept hearing the words, "Gotta get higher" and "Shut the gates."

A gate is an opening, a means of entrance. It is how something or someone comes in or how something or someone goes out. I was told I could not ascend because I had these three specific gates open. Whatever comes into my life by way of these gates being open was keeping me from experiencing an open heaven. So I took this encounter extremely seriously. I do not consider myself rebellious at all, but I was admonished by this extremely large angel to shut the gates, and I am taking his command seriously.

David prays in Psalm 119:37, *"Turn away my eyes from looking at worthless things, and revive me in Your way."*

I believe that some people even reading this encounter will have the Spirit of the Lord begin to speak about different areas in their lives. He is inviting all of us to shut some gates. When we ask for more of God, there is a cry coming from God that He wants more of us. That is how it works.

I invite you to continue along on this journey with me, as I believe it is for all of us. There are real things in this world that we watch, listen, and speak that keep worldly gates open. We unknowingly allow worthless things to take residence in our hearts and minds. I was told to close these gates if I wanted to ascend higher. This comes by the conviction of the Holy Spirit who leads and guides us closer to His presence. I am so thankful that we do have not have a condemning Spirit but a convicting Spirit who leads us into all truth.

All we have to do is listen ever so closely to the prodding of the Spirit of God, and when He says, "Turn it off," we should obey. When He says, "Shut this gate," then we must shut it.

For Thy lovingkindness is before mine eyes: and I have walked in Thy truth (Psalm 26:3 KJV).

I love the cry of King David in Psalm 101:2:

I will behave myself wisely and give heed to the blameless way——O when will You come to me? I will walk within my house in integrity and with a blameless heart (AMP).

Honestly, the mouth gate—the tongue—is by far the hardest to control and "shut." The Word of God is so clear about the tongue and our conversations. This is a real gate that God is inviting us to shut. And the good news is that if God is giving us the invitation to shut our mouth gate, then He is going to give us the grace to do it. Oh how wonderful it would be if we all spoke only encouraging and uplifting words. This is His invitation to us to go higher. Because we "Gotta get higher." You know, there's a lot to see up there!

Consider seriously these passages from the Word of God:

*If anyone among you thinks he is religious, and does not bridle his **tongue** but deceives his own heart, this one's religion is useless* (James 1:26).

*We all stumble in many ways. If anyone is never at fault in what he **says**, he is a perfect man, able to keep his whole body in check* (James 3:2 NIV).

*The **tongue** also is a fire, a world of evil among the parts of the body. It corrupts the whole person, sets the whole course of his life on fire, and is itself set on fire by hell* (James 3:6 NIV).

*David said about him: "'I saw the Lord always before me. Because He is at my right hand, I will not be shaken. Therefore my heart is glad and my **tongue** rejoices; my body also will live in hope* (Acts 2:25-26 NIV).

Chapter 35

The Justice Movement

I dedicate this dream to Lou Engle,[1] Roland and Heidi Baker,[2] Wes and Stacey Campbell,[3] Patricia King,[4] James Goll,[5] Benji Nolot,[6] and all the others across the nations whom God is raising up to be voices for justice.

God is getting ready to turn up the volume on the justice movement in the earth. Every home will hear about it. Every house of prayer and prayer movement in the earth will be lifting up the cause of the helpless. They will plead the cause of those caught up in sex slavery; they will be the voice of the unborn and the voice for the orphan crying out for God to break in and set captives free.

God hears the cries of those held captive. They are in His gaze and God has an answer. He is raising up a new move of the Nazirites. He is releasing a movement again of the long-haired ones (see Judg. 13:5). He is putting within them His burden and He is anointing the words of their mouths with power. He is shining His marvelous light in the midst of great darkness. The pleas of the captives have reached His ears, and God is listening. The justice movement is the answer to the arising cries of the captives. He is knocking on the doors of His Church and inviting all to be part of this great rescue.

I had a dream. I saw the Lord begin to stir the hearts of the fathers and mothers of the justice movement. I saw the Lord send His angelic help for those who will lead the way for justice. God is answering the cries of the helpless and raising up, in a massive way, deliverance for the captives and the unborn in the nations around the earth.

The dream began as I was watching television. I was saying to myself, *God, You are beginning to move in a mighty way in the justice movement around the world. What are You doing?*

In the dream, I began to channel surf on the television. I saw a show titled "Tell-A-Vision," so I turned up the volume.

The show was about justice. It was about the lives of the unborn children, the sex-slave industry, the poor, and the orphans worldwide. It was God's cry of liberation concerning those held captive by the hands of men and women whose sole purpose was set upon darkness.

As I watched the show, I saw the Lord begin to stir the hearts of believers to meet with the Lord and discover Heaven's strategy for this time in history. I saw the Lord raise up men and women in this hour with a single voice that would lead the way in every nation. New songs were arising in the lands concerning deliverance. I heard songs begin to fill the airwaves, even in all realms of media. These songs also were being sung within His house. They were songs of deliverance and songs of justice that opened the hearts of young and old to the burden on the Lord's heart.

I saw the Lord raise up believers in every nation and put them at the very helm of the justice movement. These He will raise up to be His voice, and a movement of justice will begin to fill the earth. These leaders were called for such a time as this. It will be their sole passion. They will think about it during the day and dream about it during the night. God is going to put His heart within these "point people" so they will feel what God feels and arise in great leadership and authority worldwide.

POINT PEOPLE FOR JUSTICE

In the dream, I saw angels being dispatched. I was taken up above the nations and saw mighty angels being sent to these point people in every nation. The cries of the captives from every single tongue and tribe have reached the ears of our Father, and He is setting His plans in place by raising up a movement of justice.

As the point people slept at night, the angels entered their rooms. The angels were white. They were big. They were tall. They glowed like shining lights, like stars. A florescent glow encircled them as they floated across each floor. Their eyes were set on the men and women they were sent to with orders from Heaven to put within these people plans from the heart of God.

They entered with a purpose and went straight to each one. I could tell the angels were sent on a mission. They had a sole purpose from Heaven to do this one thing and they were sent directly from the throne of God. Their faces were set straight ahead on the man or woman God had chosen to raise up for such a time as this—for the cries of the captives are heard day and night by our heavenly Father.

REWIRED DESIRES

As the point people slept, I noticed that the angels began to operate, to rewire desires on the inside of their human hearts and minds. The angels were sent to stir up passion and to put within these men and women the burden of the Lord. As the angels were operating on the men and women, their stomachs were literally opened up and their passions began to change. The angels were connecting different passions and cutting some out.

BURNING FIRE WITHIN

An angel came into each room with the Book of Daniel. He held it up with his right hand and lit it on fire. As the Book of Daniel burned, it was put in the stomach of each of the point people. The angel then sealed up the person's stomach with the burning fire of the Book of Daniel inside. The angels did not sew up these men and women; they were sealed up.

All over the nations, within the innermost beings of these men and women, they were on fire. Their stomachs began to burn like they had a stomachache or an ulcer. It reminded me of when the disciples were walking with Jesus and said, "Did our hearts not burn within us when He was with us?" (See Luke 24:32.)

Then one by one, the angels left each room and each sleeping man and woman. They even walked out the front door and shut it. I saw God begin to stir the Book of Daniel within these men and women and they burned with a holy fire from deep within, carrying the burden of the Lord for those held captive in the earth, for the forgotten of the earth and for the poor.

God is raising them up to be His voice. God is going to send them to kings, presidents, and leaders to speak the Word of the Lord. They will speak fearlessly the Word of the Lord and will be unstoppable in what they say. They will be the voice of the helpless and the voice of those held captive. The Lord will also give them divine strategies and expose places and covens of darkness.

Their words will be mighty like the very voice of God Himself. Their voices will carry the authority and backing of Heaven.

> *The Spirit of the Lord GOD is upon Me, because the LORD has anointed Me to preach good tidings to the poor; He has sent Me to heal the brokenhearted, to proclaim liberty to the captives, and the opening of the prison to those who are bound; to proclaim the acceptable year of the LORD, and the day of vengeance of our God; to comfort all who mourn, to console those who mourn in Zion, to give them beauty for ashes, the oil of joy for mourning, the garment of praise for the spirit of heaviness; that they may be called trees of righteousness, the planting of the LORD, that He may be glorified* (Isaiah 61:1-3).

Endnotes

1. Lou Engle, www.louengle.com.
2. Roland and Heidi Baker, www.irismin.org/p/background.php.
3. Wes and Stacey Campbell, www.beahero.org.
4. Patricia King, www.xpmissions.com.
5. James Goll, www.compassionacts.com.
6. Benji Nolot, www.exoduscry.com.

Chapter 36

Climbing Jacob's Ladder

I thank my God always concerning you for the grace of God which was given to you by Christ Jesus, that you were enriched in everything by Him in all utterance and all knowledge, even as the testimony of Christ was confirmed in you, so that you come short in no gift, eagerly waiting for the revelation of our Lord Jesus Christ, who will also confirm you to the end, that you may be blameless in the day of our Lord Jesus Christ (1 Corinthians 1:4-8)

I had a dream. I was climbing a ladder. But this ladder was not like any other one I had ever climbed. This ladder was made of pearl instead of wood or aluminum. As I began to climb, I felt how smooth, sturdy, and thick it was to my hands. There were no sharp edges; it was perfectly rounded. Light reflected off the ladder, high-lighting its swirling colors and translucent shine. The ladder was so striking that I could not take my eyes from it. My fingers felt how smooth it was. It was rounded and fit together perfectly as if it was carved out of one great pearl.

As I climbed the ladder, I remembered Jacob's ladder in Gen-esis 28, thinking to myself, *Is this what it looked like? Could this be what Jacob saw?* It had colors of light emerald, glimmering white, soft pink, soft yellow. The colors of the ladder swirled around each other as if the ladder itself had life within it.

I climbed very slowly because there was so much to take in. As I climbed higher, angels began to pass me in both directions. Some angels were climbing up and down the ladder and other angels were flying up and down through an open portal.

The ladder was large enough that I moved over to give the angels enough room to pass either way they were going. It was an extremely busy ladder. The angels were focused. They did not look at me at all; they were not even shocked that I was there. It was like I was supposed to be there. I intuitively knew the ones heading up were on their way to receive new orders and the ones coming down were going to carry out the orders they had just received.

I stood perched on the ladder and watched all of the move-ment from Heaven take place, and it was also taking place on the earth. I saw with my own eyes the plans of Heaven being carried out on the earth. Surely what I saw was *Heaven coming down.*

Something else got my attention. The angels had blue crys-tal scrolls in their hands. Some had one or two, while others had so many scrolls that it looked like they might drop them. The angels with many scrolls were carefully coming down the ladder, or slowly flying down right through the open portal, as if carrying fine crystal that was generations old.

When I finally got to the top of the ladder, I stepped over to be greeted by a man who is a great father in the faith to many in the nations. He had learned how to access heavenly places, and he was there waiting for me. He, too, was just visiting as I was, for Heaven loves guests. He leaned back in a chair and laughed, asking me, "What took you so long?" This man had spent many hours with the Lord in his lifetime and loved teaching different generations how to access heavenly places. I understood that many people would learn to climb these same steps and make their way into heavenly realms.

KNEE-DEEP IN CLOUDS

Ephesians 2:6 says, *"And raised us up together, and made us sit together in the heavenly places in Christ Jesus."*

As I began to walk, I realized that I was knee-deep in bright, reflective clouds, yet I was walking on solid pavement. I heard voices beyond me and walked in that direction. I was thinking, *Heaven is a real place. It is not just a hope. It is not just a dream—it is real. There are real things going on in Heaven.*

I continued to walk and came to our House of Prayer in Kansas City. It was filled with people who were all worshiping and praying. This room was a mirror image of the prayers of agreement on earth. This single experience helped me understand that when we pray on earth, it is as if we are standing in front of God's throne with His full attention. I saw a room full of people praying, but there were no walls and there were no ceilings. Yet as people began to pray, they were right *in* heavenly places. They were right before the throne of God. I could see that when we pray, suddenly there is no distance between Heaven and earth. It is as if we are all right before the throne of God, and God is listening just as if we were children seated upon His knee. He hears everything. Prayer is the entrance into the realm of Heaven where God listens and answers our requests. When we pray, we are right before our Father with no walls or any ceilings. It is just you and God, even in the midst of a room full of people.

JOINED IN AGREEMENT

I joined in agreement as the other intercessors prayed for America's leaders and for other leaders throughout the nations. A man stood in the front and began to pray from First Corinthians 1:5-8. I noticed that I could hear the man's voice as he prayed, but he was a faceless man. When I have had dreams where I cannot see a face, I know this is the Spirit of the Lord. The prayers—from the Holy Spirit, from those in the room, and from myself—did not stop throughout the remainder of the dream.

As the prayers continued, I saw a succession of three men representing three different decades: one man in his thirties, one in his twenties, and one in his teens. These three men stood as the point persons of three separate generational groupings, each arranged in triangular formations.

Then I saw the angel of the Lord interact with each of the three men. The first, the man in his thirties, was standing at the head of a multitude of others of the same age. He was wearing a yellow shirt with the word **Faithful** printed on it in bold, black letters. This man represented a generation of people in their thirties who have remained faithful to the Lord in the mundane things of life. In the midst of the highs and lows and when no one was looking, these 30-somethings gave themselves to the Lord, to the place of prayer, and to the study of His Word. The Lord had seen them and was affirming those in this group with the simple but powerful word *faithful*.

I saw the angel of the Lord approach the man and hold a small scroll out for him to take. The scroll read: "To the Man Called

Faithful." As the man began to unroll the scroll, his expression showed how shocked he was at what he had been given. The Lord bent down to his ear and said, "This is your own fresh revelation. Even when you thought no one was watching, you spent long hours with Me and in studying the Word. You have now been given your own voice—with this revelation, you are not an echo."

Next, I saw the man in his twenties standing as the lead of others who were the same age. They all were drummers; each one had a snare drum and drumsticks as if they were in a marching band together. Prayers from many in the room were directed toward this man and I was greatly moved to join in.

He took a seat behind a drum set. He played a new rhythm, and as he began to play, the sound drew everyone's attention. With each hit of the stick, I saw musical notations burst from the drums and float through the air. These floating notes were not the simple notes used to compose music; instead, each one was a small scroll with a rhythm and life of its own.

The angel of the Lord took one of the floating scrolls, touched the man's lips with it, and said, "That which you play with your hands is also that which you will prophesy with your mouth. You are surely more than a drummer. A mighty revival is coming, and you will play a part. You will not only play the rhythm with your hands, but you will prophesy the revelation with your mouth. There will be times when you are shot out like an arrow and times when you stay under the shadow of My wings."

Then the angel of the Lord leaned close to the man's ear and said, "All those times you prayed, saying, 'God, there has to be more than this,' well, here is the more you asked for." The Lord quickly stretched out the man's arms straight in front of him, made his hands into fists, and pushed scrolls straight through his knuckles and wrists so that they were lodged inside his forearms.

The young man's arms began throbbing and pulsing until he couldn't stay still. He began playing literal revelation and then speaking what he was playing. He seamlessly went back and forth several times between playing rhythms from Heaven and speaking Heaven's words.

This brought me to the third man, the one in his teens, who stood at the head of others the same age. This young man walked over and sat behind a piano. He began to play, prophesy, and intercede all within one song. As he began to play and sing out, his mouth turned into a musical megaphone—just like a trumpet and bigger than his entire head. The sound that came out of his mouth was powerful, confident, and rich.

The angel of the Lord approached him and began tossing many scrolls into his mouth. As he did, I could hear a sound like an alarm coming out of the young man's mouth while he sang. But it was a beautiful alarm, not the typical harsh and startling alarm sound. As he sang, a multitude of youth his age began to join in behind him. Their songs were songs of joy, freedom, and prophecy. I thought of Ezekiel 3:1-3:

> Moreover He said to me, "Son of man, eat what you find; eat this scroll, and go, speak to the house of Israel." So I opened my mouth, and He caused me to eat that scroll. And He said to me, "Son of man, feed your belly, and fill your stomach with this scroll that I give you." So I ate, and it was in my mouth like honey in sweetness.

Then each of the three groups began to sing, play new rhythms, and preach in total harmony. They preferred each other in counter-melodies, in rhythm, and in prophetic revelation. As this beautiful, unified song was woven together, fragrance began to fill the room.

THE COURTROOM

The dream abruptly switched. The type of room we were in changed into a courtroom. Jesus stood at the head of a large conference table with a wooden gavel in His right hand. He declared, "The prophets are arising. Just as the singers, musicians, and intercessors are arising, so are the prophets. What have you set in place to govern the hearts of the prophets? If you have nothing in place, this will be the outcome."

Then Jesus turned on a movie. Hundreds of messy and loud oxen ran across the screen. They were grunting, bellowing, and jostling each other, each one louder than the next, and trying to get through a small gate all at the same time. Though they were getting stuck because of the bottleneck, they kept trying to push their way through the small gate all at once. They were under compulsion—chaotic and unguarded, but without guile—to reach their destination.

Jesus asked again, "What have you set in place to govern the hearts of the prophets? They are arising." The passion in His voice showed how serious He was about governing those who carry His Word to the nations.

Of the several of us sitting at the table, no one had an answer—there was only silence. Jesus waited, giving us time to reflect and respond, but there were no adequate words.

We had no answer; we were not prepared. He had made His point.

Then Jesus said, "Meeting adjourned," and slammed the gavel down on the table one last time. With the gavel's final *crack* on the table, Jesus suddenly disappeared, and we were left staring only at the gavel lying on its side.

After a few quiet moments, one man softly said, "We have to take this seriously." I understood this final scene to mean that the Lord wanted to make sure His prophetic voices would have a safe place to be nurtured and cared for. They need a resting place, somewhere to call home, even if for a short season.

I love this dream, and as I began to ponder it, I believe there are three distinct parts to it.

Number 1: I was climbing the ladder, and I saw with my own eyes and experienced that Heaven is very interested in the earth. Heaven is a real place; it is the governmental center of all authority on the earth, under the earth, and above the earth. It is the place where God dwells. And still today, just as Jacob saw, the angels are ascending up to receive their orders and descending to carry out their orders. We see this in Genesis 28 and again in Luke 1:19; Hebrews 1:14; Psalm 103:19-23; and Psalm 104:4.

> *The Lord has made the heavens His throne; from there He rules over everything. Praise the Lord, you angels of His, you mighty creatures who carry out His plans, listening for each of His commands. Yes, praise the Lord, you armies of angels who serve Him and do His will! Praise the Lord, everything He has created, everywhere in His kingdom. As for me—I, too, will praise the Lord* (Psalm 103:19-23 NLT).

> *Who maketh His angels spirits; His ministers a flaming fire* (Psalm 104:4 KJV).

I heard a real prayer being prayed over His house from First Corinthians 1:5-7. It was the most beautiful picture of prayer. Even as we cry out the apostolic prayers from the earth, we have a great Intercessor in Heaven crying His very Word over us.

> *[So] that in Him in every respect you were enriched, in full power and readiness of speech [to speak of your faith] and complete knowledge and illumination [to give you full insight into its meaning].*

In this way [our] witnessing concerning Christ (the Messiah) was so confirmed and established and made sure in you that you are not [consciously] falling behind or lacking in any special spiritual endowment or Christian grace [the reception of which is due to the power of divine grace operating in your souls by the Holy Spirit], while you wait and watch [constantly living in hope] for the coming of our Lord Jesus Christ and [His] being made visible to all (I Corinthians I:5-7 AMP).

Number 2: The second thing I saw was the Lord beginning to stir three different generations—the teens, those in their twenties, and those in their thirties. David was anointed king as a teen and also fought and killed Goliath while in his teens. Jeremiah was in his youth when the Lord called him as a prophet (see Jer. 1:4-10). Daniel was a young teen when he was captured and taken into Babylonian captivity (see Dan. 1:3-4). It was during Daniel's teens when God, whom Daniel called "the revealer of mysteries," began to speak to him in dreams and to give him great favor. Mary, the mother of Jesus, was a teen when she was visited by God's angel. Timothy was told by Paul to let no one despise his youth (see I Tim. 4:12).

I could see in this dream that God is going to stir the hearts of our youth in a great way and literally put His Word in their hearts and minds. They will be great messengers in the earth and proclaim His mysteries even at a young age.

I saw a great army of young musicians in their twenties. He is raising up His Levites, those who can play with skill and also prophesy the Word of the Lord. I heard new rhythms and sounds and knew that these are some of the sweet psalmists God is raising up in the earth to play a new sound, to play a new rhythm, and to prophesy to the nations.

God is raising up a new breed of drummers and musicians who know the Word as well as they know their instruments. They are skilled in the Word of God and skilled on their instruments. They have been crying out, "There has to be more," and God is going to show Himself to this new breed. They shall prophesy, for they shall encounter the very God whom they are asking, "Is there more?"

Sing to Him a new song; play skillfully with a shout of joy (Psalm 33:3).

Then I saw the group of those in their thirties—those who remained faithful when no one was looking. They had been faithful for many years, and God was going to encounter them afresh. I saw a great movement of those in their thirties who for years may have felt unnoticed by those they had served with, but they are not forgotten by their Father. He is coming with a fresh word, a new insight, a fresh message. Many of these encounters and fresh words will be written into books. God is coming to visit those who have been faithful when no one was looking, for they have always been in His gaze and are the ones God has called *faithful.*

...and your Father who sees in secret will reward you openly (Matthew 6:6).

Number 3: Last I saw the heart of the Lord for His prophets, for the young ones arising and for the prophets who have spoken His Word for many years. God was asking a question. Would there be a safe place for His prophetic messengers? These are some of His favorite mouthpieces, and He is inviting pastors and apostolic leaders in the earth to provide a safe place of rest for their souls and to lead them in love.

A New Thing

I believe God is doing a new thing in the earth. Do not read this dream and think, *Oh, I'm too old* or *I'm not old enough.* He is *not only* using those in their teens, twenties, and thirties—this dream just happened to be about these three different age groups of men and women. God is using and calling forth *every* generation. The prophetic word works like this: when you read it or hear it and it makes your heart leap inside, then *take it—it's yours.* God is stirring every age group.

In Chapter 18 of this book I saw the Lord was calling the moms and dads and the grandparents to get back on the wall, for we never retire from God's purposes.

> *Behold, I will send you Elijah the prophet before the coming of the great and dreadful day of the LORD. And he will turn the hearts of the fathers to the children, and the hearts of the children to their fathers. . .* (Malachi 4:5-6).

Chapter 37

Dark but Lovely

I am dark, but lovely... (Song of Solomon 1:5).

I had a dream. In the dream, I had just returned home from work. I had worked all day long at a bank, so I was dressed in nice clothes and shoes. It had been an extremely busy day with lots of running across the bank lobby and lots of running up and down steps, so my body and my feet were tired. I came home and lay down on my bed to take a nap. I had taken off my high-heeled shoes, but I still had on my nice clothes that I had worn to work.

I remember rubbing my sore, aching feet. Now, not to be too graphic, but when I took off my shoes, my feet were throbbing, sweaty, and smelly. I glanced at my toes and noticed that my toe-nails needed to be clipped and painted.

With all those thoughts about my feet spinning around in my head, I started to go to sleep. Then, just as my eyelids were begin-ning to close, I noticed someone walk through the doorway of my bedroom. I opened my eyes and blinked a couple of times to grasp who was standing in my room. As my eyes focused, I saw this was not just any ordinary person. It was Jesus. He walked in my room like it was His own room and it seemed totally normal that He was there. I found myself suddenly awake, not tired anymore. He walked over to the foot of my bed, and He had a smile on His face. His countenance was bright.

His brown eyes were looking right at my face. They were set. He was not turning away, and He kept smiling. His hair was brown and wavy. It came down to His shoulders. But above all, I noticed the kindness in His eyes and the love on His face that was focused on me. All His attention and all His gaze was set on my face.

He did not speak. He just focused in on my eyes, never looking at anything else in the room, just gazing right into me. Just then, He turned and grabbed a chair. He pulled the chair over and sat down at the end of my bed.

When He sat down, it made me cringe as He sat right at my feet. He sat on a chair at the end of my bed and my feet, my smelly toes, were right underneath His glorious nose. I was horrified! I was thinking, *Why couldn't You sit down at my head? At least I still have my makeup on. Why did You have to sit right there at my feet?*

I was not saying anything out loud, but I was screaming to myself on the inside, and I knew Jesus understood every silent word that I was speaking only in my heart. All I could think about was how bad my feet smelled, how sweaty they were, how my toenails were unpainted and gross, and how I probably had toe-jam between each toe too!

The thoughts racing within my mind were all focused and centered on myself. All my attention turned to how imperfect my feet were and how imperfect I was. I stopped looking at Jesus, the perfect Man, at the foot of my bed and put all my attention on me in all of my imperfections—and there were many of them.

In a moment, my eyes turned from the beauty of His face. I was not looking into the beauty and brightness of His eyes. I was not focused on Him and His beauty and glory. I turned my focus to myself and kept thinking about how dark I was. I didn't even have my toenails painted, and here they were in a front row seat under the nose of the King of kings.

I thought, *Oh, I should have kept my shoes on. Oh, if I would not have laid down on my bed....* All of my thoughts were on what I should have done and what I possibly could have done.

But He was not bothered at all by this. His smile didn't fade; His gaze into my eyes didn't lessen. He was not even holding His nose, He was just there—looking at me as if He had nothing else to do but be with me.

Slowly He began to arise from the chair. His eyes never turned away from my face. His eyes never even glanced at my feet or toes; He held the constant gaze right into my eyes. He approached the head of my bed still gazing right into my eyes and held out His right hand for me to take. I grabbed His hand and He pulled me up off of the bed, and He began to twirl me around the room. He danced with me.

We Danced

I could hear music, a waltz. We were dancing all around my room, spinning and twirling. Suddenly we were outside the boundaries of time and gravity. All the furniture was removed and it was just Jesus and me in the ballroom of eternity waltzing upon the wings of the wind. There were no walls and no ceilings. Our floor was the clouds, and the music was creation.

There we danced. He laughed as He spun me around. It was as if I knew this dance; my feet knew all the correct steps. We flowed perfectly together. He was a great dance instructor as He guided my steps and twirls and spins. As we danced, always on His face was a smile and eyes that sparkled.

With one final twirl and one final gaze right into my eyes, He laid His right hand upon my heart and I was awakened—suddenly I was aware of the affections of His heart for me. He took a final bow and disappeared. I could feel myself floating right down until I was back in my bedroom standing in the very place where the dance started.

A Heart Awakening

I sensed an awakening within the depths of my heart as I had felt the kindness and gentleness of His gaze. As I began to relive our dance, I realized that Jesus had eyes only for me. When He came into my room, He was not looking at all my imperfections; He was looking at my heart. His attentions were not upon my feet or all the tiny things that I seem to make large in my life. Jesus was about one thing and that was to awaken my heart to His love for me.

As I focused upon my shortcomings, Jesus wanted to awaken within me the revelation of His love. He wanted to dance high above the clouds. He wanted to touch my heart and set His seal upon me so I would realize His love is stronger than death. His love is stronger than the grave. Nothing can quench His love, and in the middle of all my thoughts about how beautiful He was and how imperfect I was, He extended His hand to dance. I danced with my Beloved high above the clouds, waltzing on the wings of the winds and listening to the song of creation. There my feet stepped in perfect time with the King of kings.

This is the glory of what He does. When we begin to lose focus on Him and His love, when we begin to see our lack more than His love for us, Jesus reminds us of His passion and the power of His blood in our lives.

He invites us on this journey; for though we are weak—or smelly—He calls us lovely.

Chapter 38

Prophetic Song Arises

...Thus says the Lord to you: *"Do not be afraid nor dismayed because of this great multitude, for the battle is not yours, but God's.... You will not need to fight in this battle. Position yourselves, stand still and see the salvation of the LORD, who is with you, O Judah and Jerusalem!" Do not fear or be dismayed; tomorrow go out against them, for the LORD is with you."*

And Jehoshaphat bowed his head with his face to the ground, and all Judah and the inhabitants of Jerusalem bowed before the LORD, worshiping the LORD. Then the Levites of the children of the

Kohathites and of the children of the Korahites stood up to praise the LORD God of Israel with voices loud and high.

So they rose early in the morning and went out into the Wilderness of Tekoa; and as they went out, Jehoshaphat stood and said, "Hear me, O Judah and you inhabitants of Jerusalem: Believe in the LORD your God, and you shall be established; believe His prophets, and you shall prosper."

And when he had consulted with the people, he appointed those who should sing to the LORD, and who should praise the beauty of holiness, as they went out before the army and were saying: "Praise the LORD, for His mercy endures forever." Now when they began to sing and to praise, the LORD set ambushes against the people of Ammon, Moab, and Mount Seir, who had come against Judah; and they were defeated (2 Chronicles 20:15,17-22).

I had a dream. I was taken up above the earth. I was standing in the clouds and looking at the whole world, and I saw great shaking coming to the United States, Israel, China, Germany, and Europe as a whole.

As I was looking at the earth, these nations started to shake, like a violent earthquake. I felt no fear, but it was as if the Lord was giving us a heads-up. He was saying, "There is shaking coming. Get ready." I knew this was our season to dig deep in the Word, to be filled with the Word of God, to eat the scroll like Ezekiel did:

So I opened my mouth, and He caused me to eat that scroll. And He said to me, "Son of man, feed your belly, and fill your stomach with this scroll that I give you." So I ate, and it was in my mouth like honey in sweetness. Then He said to me: "Son of man, go to the house of Israel and speak with My words to them" (Ezekiel 3:2-4).

We were to feed on the Word of the Lord to have it written upon our hearts. From preachers, to teachers, to moms within the walls of their homes, to the men and women in the marketplace—everywhere a call went out to eat of and digest this Word, sing this Word, prophesy this Word, pray this Word, so that in these times of shaking we would have a song in our hearts and a prophetic cry coming from our mouths that was based upon the Word of the Lord.

Then my attention focused upon the nation of Israel. I saw the hand of God begin to stir the hearts of the leaders in the land to make a choice for protection around the borders of what is rightfully theirs. Israel began to protect its borders like a mama bear protects her cubs. Israel loves every part of what God has promised to her, even the dust from the stones:

> *You will arise and have mercy on Zion; for the time to favor her,*
> *Yes, the set time, has come. For Your servants take pleasure in her*
> *stones, and show favor to her dust* (Psalm 102:13-14).

Stand With Israel

Suddenly, I saw Israel take the reins back. The leaders of Israel began to make some decisions regarding their land and their borders. These choices caused Israel to lose some friends. When I say friends, I am speaking of nations leaving Israel's side. As Israel started making its own decisions, I saw that it was going to be costly for other nations to stand with Israel because Israel had taken the reins back, and they were making their own decisions and not following the requests of the other nations.

Israel's choices were not popular with other nations. It seemed that for those outside Israel to stand with her was to almost go against their own nations. Yet this agenda of protection rose up within the hearts of the Israeli leaders with a zeal that could not be stopped.

A SONG AND A SHAKING

Standing in the heavens, I began to hear a sound like melodies and music, which was arising like a fragrance. I saw a real mist rising from the earth, and it carried melodies right up past me to the throne of God. The melodies were beautiful. There were beautiful voices singing in major and even minor keys. I was captured by the sound of the voices.

These voices caught my attention because when I looked down, I saw blackness and darkness and confusion. But in the middle—*in the middle* of it all—was the beauty of prophetic songs and music arising like a perfume.

I heard a song like a great light in the midst of shaking and darkness; it was like water in the middle of a desert. In the midst of the shaking came direction, comfort, and hope. This was released through the prophetic songs and music. As I looked down and saw the earth, I noticed this fragrance began to arise from every place. It was not just coming from one area; it began to arise from every nation. This sweet fragrance, this beautiful sound, had authority in it even as it arose.

THE ARMY OF JUDAH

The dream shifted, and I saw a great army arising. It was the army of Judah and of the Levites—an army of prophetic singers and skilled prophetic musicians arising in the earth to sing a new song to the Lord and to declare in glory His song to the nations. It was powerful. It was loud. It was a new sound that had authority backing up the melodies that were arising.

This army was getting ready to be dispatched to the earth. Where darkness abounds, a new song will arise, and instead of hopelessness, fear, and destruction, there will be a song arising with an anointing to bring hope, direction, and comfort. I saw people in the nations begin to run to this sound as it was a sound of hope. And *in the midst* of the sound—just like in Second Chronicles—the Lord will set ambushes against darkness. The Lord will send out reminders through the prophetic song going forth that the battle is the Lord's, and He will fight for us.

It is a season for prophetic singers and musicians to *get ready.* God is really jealous right now for our tongues and our mouths because great anointing and authority is coming upon our words and voices—that which proceeds from our mouths. He desires that we would walk in Psalm 149:6-9.

Suddenly, the dream shifted, and I heard a Voice declare, "I am getting ready to release the Jehus. But their weapons will not be weapons that they carry in their hands; their weapons will be their voices. I am going to anoint their voices to speak as one. The breaker is coming upon the voice, and the Voice—God's voice— will be the weapon. These are the ones who speak in boldness and authority, and they do not shrink back but speak with precise wisdom and they speak the mind of Christ in authority. Just like Jehu arose in all boldness and zeal to fulfill the will of the Lord, so will these Jehus strike the principalities of darkness and evil. They will not stop until their mission is accomplished."

I noticed that at the sound of the Voice, everything seemed to stop, everything seemed to listen, nature itself seemed to quiet and lean into the sound of declaration coming from above. The Voice penetrated to the core of me; it almost made the bones inside my body shake. This is the Voice of many waters, the Voice that causes the cedars to break in two—and He declared that the Jehus are arising.

Their words and their songs will be in direct contrast to the direction of the world. It will be the least popular thing to say. It will be the most apolitical thing to say, but it will be the Word of the Lord. It will be the song upon His heart that is being sung out. I saw them arise in every place.

Your Invitation

Maybe you are reading this dream right now and feel a stirring of the Lord on the inside. I believe this is the Spirit of the Lord inviting you to eat the scroll, to mediate on His Word, to have His Word written upon your heart, to sing His Word, to pray His Word, and to memorize His Word.

Even as you begin to sing the Word and eat the scroll, God is inviting you to be part of this great army of Levites that He is raising up to send to the ends of the earth. For during the middle of shaking is when the songs will begin to arise in great passion, in great beauty, and in great authority.

For the Lord is good and His mercy endures forever.

Chapter 39

Catch and Snatch

The Lion of Judah is truly on the prowl for souls. He is not afraid of darkness. He loves to arise in darkness. I had this dream in the fall of 2007, and I believe we saw this literally played out with Michael Jackson. What I dreamt about two years earlier happened in the streets of Los Angeles and all around the world. I kept thinking of this dream over and over, and I knew that this weak man was with Jesus and that Heaven was rejoicing because he who was lost has now been found. This dream brought hope to my heart and to many who had read this dream, for God desires that none should perish.

The Lord is not slack concerning His promise, as some count slackness, but is longsuffering toward us, not willing that any should perish but that all should come to repentance (2 Peter 3:9).

I had a dream. I was in California walking down the streets of Hollywood, Hollywood Hills, Brentwood, Los Angeles, and Malibu. It was nighttime. When I was in L.A., the city was black, and as I looked up, I could see the stars shining. With each step I took, the very vibration from my shoes hitting the pavement seemed to say, "Time...time...time...." I began to call out Hosea 6:1, "*Come, and let us return to the LORD...*" over California, "Come...Come California. It is your time, California. It is your time to turn."

I started prophesying Hosea 2:14-16 as I was walking in the dark streets:

Therefore, behold, I will allure her, will bring her into the wilderness, and speak comfort to her. I will give her her vineyards from there, and the Valley of Achor as a door of hope; she shall sing there, as in the days of her youth.... And it shall be, in that day, says the LORD, That you will call Me "My Husband," and no longer call Me "My Master."

Suddenly, I was not walking by myself down these streets, but walking right along beside me was a real, live Lion. I was startled at first because He was so huge. I knew this was no mere lion but the *Lion of Judah.*

My whole body was hardly the length of His face, and He was on the prowl. I was very taken with this Lion. He was on a mission. It was very clear that He was only passing through, and He had no ties to this land. He was eternally minded and consumed with eternity. He was prowling the streets and gazing into the windows of people's houses. He had one thing on His mind—souls. He was looking into people's windows to see if there were any with thoughts of God and of eternity.

The streets were dark, yet His eyes were like that of an eagle. He could focus in on people right inside their homes and see their thoughts and their hearts. I followed His gaze into the windows. Then He turned to me, He got right up in my face, eye to eye, and He said, "Be watchful and know what I am doing. Catch and snatch. I am going to catch them. I am going to chase them down, and then I am going to snatch them. I am going to snatch them right into eternity." He said, "Remember this and watch for the signs. Remember to watch for the signs."

He kept saying, "I am going to lure Hollywood into the wilderness by catching the hearts of the 'idols of the land,' and I am going to snatch them into eternity in one breath."

I was very aware that I was walking the streets of L.A. with a *Lion* and this Lion was talking to me. He kept saying, "I am going to catch them and turn their hearts in one breath. And then, in an instant, I am going to snatch them into eternity. They are *Mine.* They are *Mine.*"

He continued, "It will be sudden, and the grief that will fill the very heart of L.A. will cause hearts all over to begin to look up and to begin to seek out eternity and to begin to turn. *This* is the day of salvation. This will be the day when the harvest will be ripe and ready. *This will be the day* when the harvest fields will be ripe and ready."

He said, "There have been many prophetic words about My heart for Hollywood and revival breaking out, but it will come with a price. People will not be able to explain it. It will dominate the news more than any other story.

"Let those who have ears to hear, let them hear.

"So, those who have an ear to hear, let them hear and understand, for as each one of these 'idols of the land' are snatched into eternity, though the earth will mourn, Heaven rejoices. Truly, I will lead America and the nations of the earth into the wilderness and truly it is in *this* place of mourning that they will look up and call Me 'My Husband.'

"Let those who have ears to hear, let them hear. A joyful shout will be heard throughout the halls of eternity as one by one, the idols of the land will have a change of heart.

"You will not hear of a turning of the heart; you will not hear with your ears of a turning to Jesus Christ, for I will quickly and suddenly snatch them up. But *know* this, not *one* of them will be lost into eternal darkness. So hear Me now—Heaven rejoices in these ones whom I will catch and snatch.

"Let those who have ears to hear, let them hear. I am in love with these I will catch. I am in love with these I will snatch. *They are Mine.* I am not scared of darkness. I am drawn to darkness that *Light* might explode out of darkness. For out of *darkness* there came a great Light. Heaven is rejoicing in another soul stepping into eternity.

"Let those who have ears to hear, let them hear the sound of rejoicing in Heaven, for the *prodigal sons and daughters* have come home," He said.

"The Lion of Judah—The Lord of the Harvest is on the prowl and He will not relent. He carries the harvest of souls in His very being."

So Cry out with me that God's big dream of a great harvest will be fulfilled.

Chapter 40

Free Access

Let me start this encounter by giving you a little bit of background information. Years ago when I first began to sing the prophetic song, I remember it being scary. I was in my early twenties. I was a songwriter and a worship leader, and I was used to coming to a worship service fully prepared with my song list. Then we began to sing out the prophetic song, which can be singing Scriptures or singing a prayer. Sometimes what is sung is more detailed, and it may include singing what is on the Lord's heart. The prophetic song is a beautiful part of a worship service.

Years ago I was very nervous doing this because it involves creating a melody right on the spot in front of a whole church service full of people. This was not in my comfort zone. I loved to write music and had it all memorized so that I could sing out any song that was already written. At the time, everything else was very foreign to me. My pastor knew I would get nervous, so he used to come near and put his hand right in the middle of my back during worship. Sometimes he would just touch my back with his finger, and it was like he was quietly saying, "Hey, I've got your back. Go for it."

It was just the thing that I needed to sing and soar in worship. Sometimes he would whisper in my right ear, "Sing it again. Sing about the Lamb."

This background information is very important to understand the following encounter I had with the Lord. You will see why.

REVELATION 4:1

At a Friday night service, our team was singing around Revelation 4:1:

After these things I looked, and behold, a door standing open in heaven. And the first voice which I heard was like a trumpet speaking with me, saying, "Come up here, and I will show you things which must take place after this."

Our whole worship team was wearing in-ear monitors, which are really great because the worship leader can direct the whole team by speaking into his microphone and no one in the worship service can hear, only the people wearing the in-ear monitors. Justin, my worship leader, told me to sing around Revelation 4. Earlier in the day at the International House of Prayer, we were doing the same thing and I began singing from Ephesians 2:18 and Hebrews 10:19.

For through Him we both have access by one Spirit to the Father (Ephesians 2:18).

Therefore, brethren, having boldness to enter the Holiest by the blood of Jesus (Hebrews 10:19).

I came up with this chorus:

> *I've got a free ticket.*
> *I've got free access*
> *To walk through the door.*
> *A free ticket*
> *By way of the blood*
> *The blood of the Lamb.*

So that evening, my worship leader said, "Sing that again." So I began to sing around Revelation 4:1, and I began to sing out the chorus.

I had seen our pastor standing on stage during this set, which he did frequently. I had noticed him out of the corner of my eye.

Then, to my amazement, as I continued to sing out this chorus, I felt a hand touch my back. Well, because this has not happened for 20-some years, I thought *Wow, how crazy that he is doing that again after all of these years.* I felt a hand right in the middle of my back. Then, I heard in my right ear, "Keep singing. Go back to the free access part. Sing about the blood."

I kept feeling that hand on my back and hearing over and over, "Keep singing. Keep singing...sing about the free access, sing about the blood. Go back to the free access part."

So I did, I just kept singing and singing, "Free access." Everything he told me to sing, I did.

As I sang, I could not get that voice out of my head. I kept thinking how funny it was that after all of these years, my pastor would come up again and put his hand on my back and tell me in my right ear what to sing. I just kept hearing that over and over in my mind and the feeling that I had on my back was like a burning and a tingling that would not go away.

Well, I could not get that evening out of my mind, so I went into our Web-streaming archives to watch that service again. To my total amazement, I watched myself sing "Free Access," but there was no one behind me. The whole time I watched myself on the archives, my pastor was not there at all.

THE HAND OF THE LORD

I was stunned and realized that the hand that was firmly placed on my back was the hand of the Lord. It was not the hand of a person, but the hand of the Lord Himself. The voice that I heard in my right ear was not the voice of a mere mortal, but the voice of the Lord Himself. It was His hand and it was His voice saying, "Keep singing, go back to the free access...keep singing about the free access. Keep singing about the blood."

And even as I watched this IHOP archive again, I could feel His hand right in the middle of my back, a continual reminder that we have free access—the door is open with an invitation to *come up.*

I began to study Ephesians 2:18 and also Hebrews 10:19.

In Ephesians 2, the word *access* refers to the means of approaching or entering a place. According to *Strong's*, this word is *prosagwghv* (Strong's Number 4318). It means the act of bringing to, a moving to access, approach to God.[1]

The origin for the word *prosagwghy* is *prosavgw*. The Strong's number is 4317. It means: the act of bringing to; a moving to; access, approach to God; to lead, to bring; to open a way of access, for one to God; to render one acceptable to God; to draw near to, approach.

This is so exciting because I experienced and felt His real hand on my back and heard His real voice in my ear. He wanted everyone to hear it over and over again, "You have access." It is not what you can do. It is not how good you are. This access has everything to do with what He, Jesus Christ, did for us. It is by His Spirit, who is our divine Escort to God, who brings, leads, and causes us to draw near to God.

Hebrews 10:19 reminds us also that it is by the blood of Jesus that we can enter the holiest with boldness. Again, this is what His blood has done for us; it is about the power of His blood that is so much greater than the hold of sin in our lives. It is by *His blood* that we can approach the holiest with boldness.

The word *enter*, Strong's Number 1529, is *eisodos*. It means: an entrance; the place or way leading into a place (as a gate); the act of entering. The word origin for *eisodos* is *hodos*, which means: a way; a travelled way, road; a travelers' way, journey, travelling.

This is so exciting. We have *access*. We have a divine Escort. We have an entrance to the holiest because of the blood of the Lamb. We have the act of entering because of the blood of Jesus Christ.

I was able to hear firsthand from God. I have firsthand information. I have the orders from Heaven to "Keep singing...Sing about the free access...Sing about the blood."

Some have asked, "How do you know it was His voice?" I know because it was a familiar voice. It did not surprise me, and I was not thinking, *Who is this? Who is talking to me?* The voice that spoke to me was a voice I knew. That is why I thought it was my pastor because I know his voice so well too.

Most assuredly, I say to you, he who does not enter the sheepfold by the door, but climbs up some other way, the same is a thief and a robber. But he who enters by the door is the shepherd of the sheep. To him the doorkeeper opens, and the sheep hear his voice; and he calls his own sheep by name and leads them out. And when he brings out his own sheep, he goes before them; and the sheep follow him, for they know his voice. Yet they will by no means follow a stranger, but will flee from him, for they do not know the voice of strangers (John 10:1-5).

So every day the voice of the One I love and know reminds me to: Keep singing…keep singing about the free access. Keep singing about the blood.

Beloved, this is not just my invitation. It is yours. You have free access by the divine Escort of the Spirit by way of the blood of the Lamb. I believe Heaven loves guests, and the invitation is given, the price has been paid.

> *You've got a free ticket.*
> *You've got free access*
> *To walk through the door.*
> *A free ticket, by way of the blood*
> *The blood of the Lamb*

Endnote

1. *Strong's Exhaustive Concordance.* All definitions in this chapter are from this source.

Chapter 41

The Arising Josephs

Then Joseph's master took him and put him into the prison, a place where the king's prisoners were confined. And he was there in the prison. But the LORD was with Joseph and showed him mercy, and He gave him favor in the sight of the keeper of the prison. And the keeper of the prison committed to Joseph's hand all the prisoners who were in the prison; whatever they did there, it was his doing. The keeper of the prison did not look into anything that was under Joseph's authority, because the LORD was with him; and whatever he did, the LORD made it prosper (Genesis 39:20-23).

I had a dream. I was an observer in a prison. I was not a prisoner but merely watching those who were in prison. I looked to my right and saw an angel. He handed me a pad and a pencil, and he said, "Write this down. Write down what you see." So I began to write. I sat in the corner of a dark cave and began to scribe what was in front of me. It was dark and wet with not much light. It was dreary and very oppressive. Some men were allowed to walk free, but most had chains around their ankles. The floor seemed to be made out of stone. It was cold and wet.

When the prisoners walked, the sound of chains could be heard clinking together on the stone floor. Some were actually chained to the walls, their hands and feet bound. The scene was depressing. There was a feeling of hopelessness and lack of purpose. *After all,* I thought, *this is a prison.* I was writing all of this down, and all the while the angel stood beside me watching the whole scene too.

A young man walked in front of me and something about him caught my attention. He seemed to have purpose even in the middle of those who didn't. He did not seem depressed even though everything around him was depressing. I found myself just watching him move about the prison, talking to prisoners and doing the duties set before him. He did not seem to hate his tasks. He was working, yet his countenance did not look like the others who were held captive in this same place.

The angel that was with me bent down to my right ear and said, "Do you know who that young man is?" I said, "No, I don't." I had no idea, for the heaviness of the oppression and darkness was making me depressed, and I was only the scribe in my own dream. Then the angel whispered softly, "That is Joseph."

I thought, *This is Joseph?* I should have known for he didn't look like the other prisoners. He didn't carry their hopelessness, their anger, or their lack of destiny. The angel I was with suddenly held a Bible in his right hand, and he turned to Genesis 39:20-23. This passage was highlighted, and I began to read. This was the second time Joseph was thrown in prison and still he had hope and he walked with purpose, even to the point where Joseph was the one given all authority under the keeper of the prison. Yet there was a deep humility about this young man. He was broken but not crushed in spirit. And in this dark and dreary place, what surrounded this young man was the presence of God.

From Prison to Palace

At this point, the angel I was with leaned down and said, "Take note. This is the message. This is the place where many people give up. They are only in the middle of their journeys and yet they allow their current circumstances to govern their emotions. They may be pressed down and crushed from every side, but they need to turn their eyes upward. For there is coming a mighty shift in the earth, and a clarion call for the Josephs will arise. And just like Joseph in the Old Testament, there are those who are appointed to arise in the earth, from the prison to the palace in one day."

Suddenly, the scene changed and I could see men and women in the middle of living their lives who felt just like Joseph in the Old Testament. I could see those who felt like they were in their own prisons of life. But just like Joseph, these were prisons of God's making, for God had set up their circumstances so that He could show Himself strong right in the middle of where they were in life.

In this dream I saw some who felt their work or their jobs seemed trivial; they knew they were created for great things in God and yet they felt caught in mundane jobs, or jobs seeming to go nowhere. Some people I saw were being caught in false accusations in life and trying to not be offended. I felt specifically this dream was about the marketplace men and women, those with smaller businesses who sweat to bring in every single penny.

Suddenly, I was brought into today and I watched men and women who seemed to be in their own prisons. They were walking with hopelessness and lack of destiny. I saw that they were like the other prisoners in Joseph's prison and not like Joseph who walked and worked with purpose.

NEW HOPE

I had a new hope in my heart and I wanted to shout and encourage our marketplace men and women and our stay-at-home moms and dads. I wanted to encourage those who feel beat down and overlooked, and tell them that it is not the end of their stories.

I wanted tell them, "Listen, you are only in the middle of your chapter. There is a whole book laid out in front of you. Do all that you can do in this season. Find the Lord and go after His presence in *this* season. It is a necessary season to find His presence in the places where you are pressed down."

In the dream I saw Joseph in prison after he was falsely accused. As I have studied the life of Joseph, this key about Joseph is said best by Matthew Henry:

> We have him here a sufferer, falsely accused (v. 13-18), imprisoned (v. 19-20), and yet his imprisonment made both honourable and comfortable by the tokens of God's special presence with him (v. 21-23). And herein Joseph was a type of Christ, "who took upon him the form of a servant," and yet then did that which made it evident that "God was with him," who was tempted by Satan, but overcame the temptation, who was falsely accused and bound, and yet had all things committed to his hand.

Those that have wisdom and grace have that which cannot be taken away from them, whatever else they are
robbed of. Joseph's brethren had stripped him of his
coat of many colors, but they could not strip him of
his virtue and prudence.... Those that can separate us
from all our friends yet cannot deprive us of the gra-
cious presence of our God. When Joseph had none of
all his relations with him, he had his God with him.
Joseph was separated from his brethren, but not from
his God; banished from his father's house, but the Lord
was with him, and this comforted him.[1]

I woke up from this dream and knew these Josephs were created for such a time as this with great wisdom and a supernatural
strategy from the Lord.

They have been hidden away and, in an instant, God is going
to put them before kings and presidents. But the season in prison
is part of the testimony. This is the place of encounter, and this is
the place of reaching for the presence of God and calling on His
name. This is the place to learn to hear His voice. This is the place
to not be offended.

In the middle of it all is where we prepare. No one is out of the gaze
of our God. He is the One who gives wisdom and knowledge and
strategy. This is a *now time* to ask for the strategy of Heaven because
God will send out His Josephs to take care of the crisis. The great
switch is getting ready to take place on the earth.

God's Josephs will be let out of their prisons to lead a nation
away from famine and to speak to leaders, kings, and presidents.
What worked before will not work in the future. God has set it
up so we need Him. The wise men and women of the earth with
knowledge of economics and finance will not be able to solve all
the problems because God is doing a new thing—and when God
shifts, we have to shift with Him. I have heard it said that "small

is the new big" regarding financial issues. I believe that the Lord is going to surround small business owners with great favor, and their words and advice will be heard by nations.

WITHOUT OFFENSE

So do what you have before you to do in all honesty and without offense. I saw clearly in my dream that Joseph was not offended at his situation; he found God there. Therefore, when the Lord opened the prison door, Joseph did not come out with an offended and angry heart. Instead, he spoke words of wisdom because even in prison, he had been with his God.

Josephs, get ready.

ENDNOTE

I. *Matthew Henry's Commentary.*

Chapter 42

Abiding in the Vine

I do not pray for these alone, but also for those who will believe in Me through their word; that they all may be one, as You, Father, are in Me, and I in You; that they also may be one in Us, that the world may believe that You sent Me. And the glory which You gave Me I have given them, that they may be one just as We are one: I in them, and You in Me; that they may be made perfect in one, and that the world may know that You have sent Me, and have loved them as You have loved Me (John 17:20-23).

I had a dream. In my dream, I woke up and I saw eyes looking right straight into my eyes. It was as if someone was within one inch of my face, just looking right into my eyes. It was startling to wake up in the middle of the night and see eyes looking straight into mine. My heart began to beat rapidly in my chest; I gasped for air because I was so surprised. The face of these eyes was so very close to my face, I felt His breath. The white of His eyes glowed almost as if the whites were florescent and the pupils were so clear.

Then I heard a voice, "I want to show you something. I want to show you the meaning of *abiding*. I want to show you the power you have by simply abiding." It was the Lord. My heart began to slow down. My Friend had come.

I rose from my bed and started following Jesus. Suddenly I realized that I was not in my own house anymore; I was walking down a long hallway. What got my attention was the reflection of myself with every step. I was in a house of mirrors. I was walking in a maze of mirrors. I could see the front of me, the side of me, the top of me, the back of me, and a sideward glance of me. I could see myself from every direction and from every possible angle. I could see every turn of my body; I could see every expression on my face. I could see myself in every way, every step that I took. I was lost in this maze of mirrors until I heard the gentleness of His voice on the inside.

"Keep walking. I am giving you a view from My eyes, for My eyes are everywhere." I thought, *Oh my gosh, duly noted: His eyes see everything.*

He always finds a way to remind me that He sees everything. Nothing is hidden from His gaze that roams the earth. He sees everything. He hears everything. I am under His constant gaze.

> *And there is no creature hidden from His sight, but all things are naked and open to the eyes of Him to whom we must give account* (Hebrews 4:13).

For the eyes of the LORD run to and fro throughout the whole earth, to show Himself strong on behalf of those whose heart is loyal to Him... (2 Chronicles 16:9).

Then Jesus appeared again out of nowhere. It was just me and a maze of mirrors, then Jesus was standing there. He stood in front of me and said, "Keep walking." I slowly started walking, but He was only a few steps in front of me, so I began to turn so I could walk around Him. He touched my left arm and said, "No, keep walking straight. Step into Me."

STEP INTO ME

I was a little confused and I thought, *How do I do that?* Jesus, knowing my thoughts and looking intently into my eyes, said again, "Keep walking straight. Step into Me."

So I did. I stepped into Christ! I mean I walked right into *Him.* I was *in* Christ. My hands, my fingers were inside Jesus Christ's hands. Every part of me was *inside* the person of Jesus Christ. I was walking with His feet. I was talking with His mouth. I was singing with His voice. I stepped *into* Christ (see John 17:20-23; Rom. 8:11).

I saw and felt what it looks like to be *in* Christ.

In the dream there was a mirror in front of me, and I looked into the mirror and I saw myself in the body of Jesus. But then all of a sudden, as I looked in the mirror, Jesus was in *me.* There was a switch. It was my body that was now on the outside, but I could see Jesus filling every crevice of who I am. It was like I was see-through, and as I looked at *my hands,* I could *see Jesus in me* with my eyes. As I walked around the room, I saw and was aware that He was in me. *His* hands were completely filling *my* hands.

When He is *in* us by His Spirit, His desire is to *fill us completely* so we are truly filled in every area—we are filled to the full measure with Christ, like filling a glass with water. Water fills the glass—there are no sections of the glass that the water cannot fill; water *fills* the glass.

In the dream, I was aware that Jesus was in me no matter what I did. Everything I watched, everything I did with my hands, everything I spoke, Christ was in me. This is my hope of glory.

I felt as if I was living and seeing a picture of Isaiah 66:1:

Thus says the LORD: "Heaven is My throne, and earth is My footstool. Where is the house that you will build Me? And where is the place of My rest?

Oh, I could feel in that moment how Jesus longs to dwell within the sanctuary of His people. This is His dwelling place. We are the temples of the Sprit of the Lord. He longs to dwell within us. We are filled with God Himself. I saw a picture of First Corinthians 3:16.

Do you not know that you are the temple of God and that the Spirit of God dwells in you?

There is a real person who is alive on the inside of us. He is *in us* and at the same time we are *in Him*.

Or do you not know that your body is the temple of the Holy Spirit who is in you, whom you have from God, and you are not your own? (I Corinthians 6:19).

I could see that every action and choice that I made, I was not alone; Jesus was with me. I was never alone, and He filled every part of me. As I began to pray, He was praying too. As I stretched out my hands, I could see His hands within mine. I am not my own. I am His, and He is mine.

You Are *in* Us, and We *in* You

This is what John 17 looks like when Jesus prays to the Father, *"I in them, and You in Me; that they may be made perfect in one."*

When I stretch out my hands to pray for someone, these are the hands of Jesus. When I touch the poor of the earth, it is His love and His passion in me. When I choose to love the one person that He puts before me, it is You, Jesus, loving that person through me.

Oh, may we ever be aware of this intimate relationship, that we know a real Man is living and alive in the depths of us who beckons us to make good choices, who beckons us to love and pray for the sick and prophesy, who continually says, "Where is the place of My rest?"

Oh, Lord, let it be in us. Let our bodies be the sanctuaries of Your Spirit that are alive every second of every minute of every hour of every day. *You are in us, and we are in You.*

Chapter 43

SOS Mountain

...Behold, he comes leaping upon the mountains, skipping upon the hills. ...My beloved spoke, and said to me: "Rise up, my love, my fair one, and come away. For lo, the winter is past, the rain is over and gone. ...The time of singing has come..." (Song of Solomon 2:8,10-12).

I had a dream. It was the middle of the night, and I was sleeping. I was awakened by the sound of someone walking on my floor, like footsteps on carpet. I sat up in bed and was suddenly wide awake as I saw Jesus at the foot of my bed in a way I had not seen

Him before. I went from being sound asleep to wide awake in ten seconds with the feeling of a weighty presence in the room.

What caught my attention were His eyes, for they were on fire. He did not have pupils—there was just fire. He did not blink; there was just fire. Looking into His eyes was like looking into a consuming fire, as if I was looking straight into *desire,* and I could see it by looking at the fire in His eyes. This is what all-consuming passion looks like; His eyes were fueled by passion itself. He did not blink, for I was looking into a fire incapable of dying out.

I could even hear the sound of the flames right in my bedroom. I seemed to be standing right in the midst of a bonfire, and the flames were flaring out of the sockets of His eyes. The fire in His eyes was focused at me. His gaze captured my every move.

Rise Up and Come Away

Suddenly, He spoke, "Rise up and come away." Then, as fast as those words were spoken, He was gone. And I asked myself, *Come away, where?*

As if I answered my own question, I was instantly transported to the very bottom, the very crevice of a mountain—not the foothills, but a great mountain. As I looked up, I could not even see the top I was so far down.

Suddenly, right before me again was Jesus saying, "Come up here." Then He was gone. Just as fast as He said, "Come," I was left again at the base of the mountain.

I was at the foot of the largest, scariest, blackest, most rugged mountain I had ever seen. With my natural eyes this mountain looked horrid and black. I thought if I tried to climb this mountain, I would surely die on it. There was *no way* to climb it. It was like I was at the bottom of a deep pit in the Swiss Alps and I could look up and see how high and rugged the mountains were.

It seemed I was in two different places at the same time, for I was standing at the very base of this mountain, yet my eyes could see Him leaping at the very top of it. I could hear His voice over and over, "Come up here."

Yet, I was down in a crevice of the mountain. I was in a deep ravine, but I could look up and see Jesus leaping from mountaintop to mountaintop. I never imagined the mountain to be this big and rugged, and I never imagined the Lord leaping so high, springing from mountaintop to mountaintop. It was as if I was up close watching Him leap but still far away.

I could see His golden feet, springing ever so precisely on the tops of the mountains. With a bound from peak to peak, He always placed His feet in the right place, never falling, never stumbling. His golden feet were pouncing alone from peak to peak, accompanied always with His invitation, "Come up, come away. It is time to sing."

It did not make sense to me. The picture of Jesus leaping from peak to peak and calling me to "come up," and my eyes seeing this rugged mountain and watching Jesus leap at the top and then saying, "It is time to sing." It did not compute in my brain. This mountain was not a little hill. It was Pike's Peak. It was Mount Everest.

The mountain looked like death. To hike up this mountain would be to surely die. He was not coming down to get me, but instead extended the constant invitation to "Come up." He seemed to be jumping with great ease from peak to peak and at the same time saying, "Sing from up here. It is time to come up and sing from up here."

Although my mind was not able to make sense of this scenario, I started the journey and kept my eyes focused on the next step. I could not look at the height of the mountain or the width of it, but I could look at the next step, the step that was before me. And all the while, I heard the constant voice in my ears, "Come up here. Sing from up here. It's time."

IT IS TIME TO SING

In the midst of my climb, I woke up. I began to ponder the greatness of these mountains and all of the songs that were written about them. This is a song that needs to be sung in a minor key—for these mountains looked like death.

When I remember this dream and when I think of these mountains, I am not seeing the foothills in Missouri or Kansas. I see the Rockies in Colorado, and I am at the very crevice between two mountains looking up to the top. Jesus is leaping, and He is soaring high in the sky, and He is yelling, "Come, come on up. It is time to sing!"

There is no way to climb this mountain. To climb it is to die. It would be like climbing Mount Everest without training. I would die.

I am wondering if this mountain is a picture of who we will be at the end of our journey—as in Song of Solomon chapter 2 when the Shulamite sees her Beloved leaping and skipping over the hills and she hears the invitation to come up. As she looks at the heights of the mountains and the ruggedness of the climb, she actually says no to His invitation. Her answer is in verse 17, "*Until the day breaks and the shadows flee away, turn, my Beloved, and be like a gazelle or a young stag upon the mountains of Bether.*"

In essence, she says to Him, "You go. You go and leap upon the mountains. I'm staying here; this is where I'm comfortable."

After seeing this mountain in my dream, I am wondering, *Could this mountain possibly be a picture of what she will be doing at the end of the journey?* It is not for her to climb in chapter 2, but it is to stir her up to hunger and thirst so that in the beginning of chapter 3 she *gets up.*

I am wondering if this mountain is mostly about God showing her who she is going to be at the end of the day. It is a little about compromise, but it is mainly about God saying, "You may not be able to do this now, but at the end of the day, this is who you are. At the end of the day, this is who you are."

I am wondering if this mountain can be compared to God calling us at the beginning of our journeys. If the Shulamite would have climbed the mountain in chapter 2, there would be no "rest of the story."

I am wondering if it is comparable to the beginning of Gideon's calling. When God called Gideon, in the beginning, before Gideon did anything, God called him a "mighty man of valor."

And the Angel of the LORD appeared to him, and said to him, "The LORD is with you, you mighty man of valor!" (Judges 6:12)

Or when Jesus called Peter out and said, "This is who you are, Peter."

And I also say to you that you are Peter, and on this rock I will build My church, and the gates of Hades shall not prevail against it (Matthew 16:18).

Or how about Esther:

...Do not think in your heart that you will escape in the king's palace any more than all the other Jews. For if you remain completely silent at this time, relief and deliverance will arise for the Jews from another place, but you and your father's house will perish. Yet who knows whether you have come to the kingdom for such a time as this? (Esther 4:13-14).

I am wondering if the whole reason the Shulamite gets out of bed and gets up in the middle of the night in Song of Solomon chapter 3:1 is because her heart is so longing and hungry because she could not go in chapter 2.

When God puts something on your heart to do and you are scared and you don't do it, then you are sick inside that you didn't.

Song of Solomon 3:1 is the turning point in the journey. The first two chapters are the foundation where she is sitting in His chambers, sitting at His table, sitting in the shade. But where she actually gets up and starts her own day-by-day journey is chapter 3.

She gets up. She starts walking. "I will arise now" is the first action verb indicating that she is not just sitting down; she is walking step by step.

And during the remainder of the story of Song of Solomon, she is actually slowly walking up the mountain in chapter 2 that she thought she couldn't climb.

Standing on the Peak

The Shulamite woman doesn't even realize she is climbing because she is taking her day-by-day, step-by-step, choice-by-choice, and yes-by-yes journey in God, one day at a time and one step at a time.

And at the very end of the journey in chapter 8, she is standing upon the very peak of the mountain that she saw in Song of Solomon 2. Then it is Jesus who comes to her and says, *"Make haste, my beloved, and be like a gazelle or a young stag on the mountains of spices"* (Song of Sol. 8:14).

Now there is nothing to do but jump. She can look behind her and actually see her history in God and remember His faithfulness. She looks back down the mountain and the only thing left to do is jump.

Ready to Leap and Reign Victoriously

Now she is ready to leap. Now she is ready to reign.

This dream is our invitation to get up out of our comfortableness and start hiking up the mountain step by step and yes by yes. Just take the next step that is in front of you. Just do it. This mountain looks like death because we must pick up our crosses and deny our flesh.

And he who does not take his cross and follow after Me is not worthy of Me. He who finds his life will lose it, and he who loses his life for My sake will find it (Matthew 10:38-39).

For our Beloved calls:

...Rise up, My love, My fair one, and come away. For lo, the winter is past, the rain is over and gone. The flowers appear on the earth; the time of singing has come, and the voice of the turtledove is heard in our land. ...Rise up, My love, My fair one and come away! (Song of Solomon 2:10-13)

The invitation has been given.

What is your response?

About Julie Meyer

Julie Meyer is a longtime and beloved worship leader and songwriter at the International House of Prayer in Kansas City. She is a prophetic singer who carries the glory and the presence of God as an abandoned worshipper. Her passion is His presence as she trumpets the message of the Bridegroom searching for His Bride!

She is the author of *Invitation to Encounter*, a recording artist with several CDs. She has traveled the world leading worship and speaking on the hearing the voice of God, sharing her encounters with the Lord, and encouraging the body of Christ to dream

Other Products by Julie Meyer

CDs:

I Fall In Love
You Make Me Smile
Better Than Life
Longing For The Day

Paint Your Picture
God Is Alive

Available at www.juliemeyer.com

In the right hands, This Book will Change Lives!

Most of the people who need this message will not be looking for this book. To change their lives, you need to put a copy of this book in their hands.

> *But others (seeds) fell into good ground, and brought forth fruit, some a hundred-fold, some sixty-fold, some thirty-fold* (Matthew 13:8).

Our ministry is constantly seeking methods to find the good ground, the people who need this anointed message to change their lives. Will you help us reach these people?

> *Remember this—a farmer who plants only a few seeds will get a small crop. But the one who plants generously will get a generous crop* (2 Corinthians 9:6).

EXTEND THIS MINISTRY BY SOWING
3 BOOKS, 5 BOOKS, 10 BOOKS, OR MORE TODAY,
AND BECOME A LIFE CHANGER!

Thank you,

Don Nori Sr., Founder
Destiny Image
Since 1982

DESTINY IMAGE PUBLISHERS, INC.

*"Speaking to the Purposes of God for This Generation
and for the Generations to Come."*

Visit our new site home at
www.DestinyImage.com

Free Subscription to DI Newsletter

Receive free unpublished articles by top DI authors, exclusive
discounts, and free downloads from our best and newest books.
Visit www.destinyimage.com to subscribe.

Write to: Destiny Image
              P.O. Box 310
              Shippensburg, PA 17257-0310

Call: 1-800-722-6774

Email: orders@destinyimage.com

For a complete list of our titles or to place an order
online, visit www.destinyimage.com.